H. B. Grant

Drill Tactics for Select Knights of A. O. U. W.

containing school of the knight, division and battalion - sword manual - rules for

camps, parades, competitive drills

H. B. Grant

Drill Tactics for Select Knights of A. O. U. W.
containing school of the knight, division and battalion - sword manual - rules for camps, parades, competitive drills

ISBN/EAN: 9783337286750

Printed in Europe, USA, Canada, Australia, Japan

Cover: Foto ©Andreas Hilbeck / pixelio.de

More available books at **www.hansebooks.com**

DRILL TACTICS

FOR

SELECT KNIGHTS

OF

A. O. U. W.

CONTAINING

SCHOOL OF THE KNIGHT, DIVISION AND BATTALION;
SWORD MANUAL; RULES FOR CAMPS, PARADES,
COMPETITIVE DRILLS; RECEPTION AND ES-
CORT DUTIES, KNIGHTLY COURTESIES,
TOGETHER WITH BURIAL SERVICE,
ETC.

Prepared under Authority of the Supreme Legion,

BY

H. B. GRANT,
Author of Grant's Knights Tem

CINCINNATI:
THE PETTIBONE M'F'G COMPANY.
1883.

Entered according to Act of Congress, in the year 1883, by
THE PETTIBONE MANUFACTURING COMPANY, Cincinnati, Ohio,
in the Office of the Librarian of Congress,
at Washington, D. C.

Select Knights, Attention!

This Manual of Military Drill, published by the Pettibone M'f'g Co., of Cincinnati, is the regulation Drill Tactics for the Select Knights, and no other should be used in our organization, and none are genuine unless they bear the impression of the Seal of the Supreme Legion upon the title page.

Fraternally, in

E. I. AND U.,

CLARK D. KNAPP,

Supreme Commander.

PREFACE.

This system of drill is so closely assimilated to those prepared by the Author for other semi-Military Orders, as well as to the U. S. Infantry Tactics, that any one familiar with either will feel little embarrassment in comprehending and using the other.

Societies often experience great difficulty in assembling a sufficient number of members to make a creditable appearance; hence, a formation with *four* as the unit is not deemed best to secure the most satisfactory results. Considering the meager number, of even moderately well-drilled men, who can usually be induced to report for society "parades"—*three* has been selected as the unit, and this appears, heretofore, to have met with general approval; because it gives the greatest display with the fewest number. If the numbers are such as to warrant a wider column (a rare occurrence), subdivisions may be formed by doubling the front, by double rank formation, or both.

In the Army, *file closers* are essential, among other measures, to preserve the integrity and effectiveness of a line in action. No such reasons obtain in uniformed societies Besides, the file closers diminish the length of the line by drafts from the body ; and detract from the shapeliness of the column by giving it a "ragged" appearance. Again they interfere, somewhat, with display movements which have become popular, hence file closers have been dispensed with.

To still further utilize every available uniform, and avoid other objectionable features for a civic society, subordinate officers are posted in the line and serve as guides—except on the few occasions when they are needed as chiefs of subdivisions.

Such arrangements have heretofore met with the favorable opinions of skilled tacticians; and intimate acquaintance with the use of these means, adopted to "swell the ranks" in public demonstrations, confirm the conviction as to correctness of the theory advanced.

From what has been said of file closers, it is deemed expedient to merge the subordinate officers in the line.

In recent publications, the author's illustrations from other works have been used without authority.

Contents.

Preface ....
Indorsement ....
Nomenclature 9, 10
School of the Select Knight 11
Manual of the Sword 26
Silent Manual 38
Salutes 14, 28, 29, 39
School of the Officer 40
School of the Legion 44
Legion and Display Drill 74
School of the Battalion 140
Honors paid by Select Knights 169
Visitation and Courtesies without Arms ... 170
Escorts of Honor 171
Reception and Escorts of Grand Officer ... 172

Dress Parade	173
Review	177
General Parade	180
Sword Signals	184
Bugle Signals—33 Signals, 1 March	186
Award of Prize and Rules for Competitive Drill	195
Camps and Camping	199
Correspondence and Orders	202
APPENDIX—Burial Service	208

Vocabulary of Military Terms.

ABOUT. A wheel (or face) of 180°. *Full about;* a wheel of 360°.

BATTALION. Two or more legions as prescribed.

CADENCE. The rate of regular planting of the feet in marching and succession of motions in the manual.

COLUMN. A number of subdivisions formed in lines one behind the other.

COLUMN OF FILES. A single or double rank faced to the right or left (into column).

COVER. Files or guides cover when exactly behind or in rear of each other, marching or at a halt.

DEPLOY. To extend; a column "extended" into line.

DISTANCE. Space between Knights or subdivisions, measured in depth (perpendicular to their front).

DIVISION. One-half (one-third or one-fourth) more or less of the legion. (In the army drill, called *Platoon*).(See p 46).

DOUBLE SECTION. Twelve Knights in line, single or double rank.

DRILL CORPS. A portion of the legion, with a head and members, organized for drilling.

ECHELON. Subdivisions in lines at equal distances, like stair steps, one more advanced than the other.

FACING DISTANCE is such that in facing to the right or left, into line, the elbows will touch.

FILE. A Knight in rank. Two or more Knights, one behind the other, in ranks.

FILE-LEADER. The Knight in front of the file, whom the others of the file *cover*.

FLANK. Either extremity of line or side of a column.

INTERVAL. Space between Knights or subdivisions in line, measured parallel to their front.

LEGION DISTANCE. A distance equal to the front of the legion when in line.

LINE. Knights formed abreast; that is, elbow to elbow.

MARCHING FLANK. The extremity of the line farthest from the pivot in the wheelings.

MOTION. A distinct movement in the manual of the sword, without pause, and designated as *first motion, second motion, etc.*

PIVOT. The Knight on the flank upon whom the wheeling is made.

POINT OF REST. The point where the right will rest in movements from right to left, or where left will rest when movement is from left to right.

POST. Position or place prescribed.

RANK. A number of Knights in line.

RIGHT IN FRONT is when the original of the line is the head of the column. The reverse is *left in front.*

ROSTER. List of Officers and Knights for duty.

SCHEDULE. A programme containing the movements, etc., to be executed.

SECTION. Six knights in line, single or double rank.

SQUAD. A small detachment of Knights. It may be used as preparatory, in lieu of Knights.

STANDARD GUARD. The Recorder, Standard Bearer and Treasurer, formed in the order named, from the right.

SUBDIVISION. Threes, sectons, etc.; a legion subdivided.

WHEEL. A circular movement by which a line of two or more Knights is placed at right angles to its former position.

WHEELING DISTANCE is such that in wheeling into line the subdivisions will exactly join those on the right and left; or the distance between subdivisions equal to the front of the subdivision.

WING. One-half of a line. One of the Grand Divisions into which a line may be divided.

School of the Select Knight.

INTRODUCTION.

The instruction of Select Knights in the drill can only be perfected by joining theory to practice.

A competent officer should be detailed to drill the Knights in the School of the Select Knight before they are permitted to enter the ranks of the legion. Stated times for drill, faithfully improved, are essential to success. A well-disciplined legion will rarely be troubled about a "constitutional number" at its meetings, and a legion that is not well drilled, cannot perform the ceremonies with credit, as deficiency in drill necessarily detracts from their beauty and impressiveness. Let those who are skeptical witness the difference before criticising.

In this work commands are given for the execution of movements toward both right and left flanks, but the explanation of the movement toward one flank only will be made. To obtain the explanation toward the other flank, substitute *left* for *right*, or the reverse.

The last syllable of a command determines its prompt execution.

The Commander has the right, and ought to command in person. But if, being present, he places temporarily in command, one who is peculiarly fitted for the position, it ought to be cheerfully acquiesced in.

When commands are prescribed herein without mention as to who should give them, it will be understood that they are given by the officer in charge.

The movements and commands in the School of the Select Knight apply with equal force in other parts of this work wherever instruction to the contrary is not given, substituting *legion*, etc., for Sir *Knights* or *Squad*.

COMMANDS.

Commands should be given in a clear, animated tone, every syllable distinct, and loud enough to be heard without difficulty by every Knight under instruction. If the lines are subdivided, the commands may be briskly repeated by the officers in charge of subdivisions, if necessary, in a lower tone, but loud enough to be heard by their particular section or division. The failure of a single Knight to understand the command may throw the entire line into confusion.

Commands are of two kinds:

1. *Preparatory;* such as *forward*, *carry*, etc., [printed in *italics*] indicate the movement to be executed.

2. Of *execution;* such as MARCH, SWORDS, etc., [printed in SMALL CAPITALS] pronounced in a firm, brief tone, indicate the exact instant for commencing, and causes the execution of a movement.

A preparatory command should always precede and be understood before adding that of execution. The cadence of commands is determined by the step. Ordinarily the cadence, at a halt, is *common time* (*p.* 16).

POSITION.

Heels on the same line, as near each other as the formation of Knight will permit. If one heel be in the rear of the other, one shoulder will be thrown back, and the position is constrained. Men knocked-kneed, or with large calves cannot, without constraint, make their heels touch while standing.

The *feet* turned out equally, forming with each other an angle of about sixty degrees. If one is turned out more than the other, the shoulders will be deranged; if both are turned out too much, the upper part of the body cannot be inclined forward without making the position unsteady.

The *knees* straight, without stiffness. If stiffened constraint and fatigue will be unavoidable.

The *body* erect upon the hips, inclining a little forward. This gives equilibrium to the position. The reverse is common—that is, throwing the shoulders back and projecting the belly, which causes inconvenience in marching, and fatigue.

The *shoulders* square and falling equally. Many have a bad habit of dropping one shoulder. Correct it at once.

The *arms* hanging naturally;

The *elbows* near the body;

The *palms* of the *hands* truned slightly to the front, hands open, fingers together and nearly straight, the little fingers behind the seams of the pantaloons. These prevent Knights from occupying unnecessary space in ranks, and tends to keep the shoulders in.

The *head* erect and square to the front;

The *chin* slightly drawn in, without constraint. Stiffness in these positions will be communicated to other parts of the body, giving pain and fatigue.

The *eyes* straight to the front, striking the ground at about the distance of fifteen yards. The surest way to keep the shoulders in line and head erect. Insist upon it.

When the Knights appreciate the importance and understand the details of the position—the *alpha* of the tactics—pass to the next lesson.

Let the Knights rest often, for a few moments at a time, until they become easy in their *positions;* for this purpose, command;

REST.

All are now at liberty to stand, sit, or lie down, but not to move more than two or three yards away, nor is silence required.

SCHOOL OF THE SELECT KNIGHT.

Wishing to relieve the attention merely, command:

1. *In place.* 2. REST.

The immobility or silence need not then be preserved, but the left heel ought to be kept in its place.

1. *Sir Knights* (or *Squad*). 2. ATTENTION.

At the first command quiet is restored, and at the second, every Knight promptly takes his position, remains motionless and fixes his attention.

To dismiss the squad, command.

1. *Break ranks.* 2. MARCH.
1. *Eyes* RIGHT (or LEFT). 2. FRONT.

At the command *right*, each Knight will turn his head promptly, but gently, so as to bring the inner corner of the left eye on a line with the center of the body, the eyes fixed on the eyes of the Knights in, or supposed to be in, the same rank. (This is the position of head and eyes in *right dress*, except that the Knight on the extreme right does not turn the head, but remains at *attention*). Retain this position until the command *front* is given, when the head and eyes resume the habitual position.

Eyes left is exactly the reverse of *eyes right*.

See that every motion is understood and properly executed before passing to the next; but do not dwell too long upon any one, lest a dislike be engendered for the work at the beginning. Be clear and plain in every explanation, and, if necessary, cause each Knight by himself to execute the motions, and correct any defect as soon as discovered. While courtesy is extended to all, *the discipline in ranks should be impartially rigid.*

SALUTES WITH THE HAND.

1. *Right* (or *left*) *hand.* 2. SALUTE.

First motion. Raise the right hand till the tips of the fingers touch the vizor opposite the right eye, thumb closed,

SCHOOL OF THE SELECT KNIGHT.

fingers and hand extended in prolongation of the forearm, elbow down. *Second motion.* Lower the hand briskly to the right until the points of the fingers are at the height of the shoulder and in front of it, elbow advanced, hand and fingers still extended in prolongation of the forearm. *Third motion.* Drop the hand to the side.

When in uniform, the proper salute should not be omitted, but the etiquette of Knightly courtesy strictly observed. This should be impressed upon the minds as other lessons are taught, by theory and practice.

A junior officer or Knight addressing a senior salutes first, which is always acknowledged. If the senior officer addresses a junior officer or Knight, the inferior in rank makes the first salute.

If the sword is in the scabbard, the salute is with the hand.

1. *Right* (or *left*). 2. FACE.

At the command *face*, raise the right foot slightly, face to the right, turning on the left heel, the left toe slightly raised; replace the right heel by the side of the left and on the same line.

The facings to the left are executed on the same heel as the facings to the right.

1. *Sir Knights.* 2. ABOUT. 3. FACE.

At the command *about*, turn on the left heel, bring the left toe to the front, carry the right foot to the rear, the hollow opposite to, and three inches from, the left heel, the feet square to each other. At the command *face*, raise the toes a little, turn on both heels, and face to the rear. When the face is nearly completed, raise the right foot and replace it by the side of the left.

1. *Parade.* 2. REST.

This gives rest, imposing both steadiness and attention.

At the command *rest*, carry the right foot three inches directly to the rear, the left knee slightly bent; clasp the hands in front of the center of the body, the left hand uppermost, the left thumb clasped by the thumb and forefinger of the right hand.

1. *Sir Knights.* 2. ATTENTION.

Resume the position of a Knight in line.

THE STEPS.

The length of the direct step in *common* and *quick time* is twenty-eight inches, measured from heel to heel.

The cadence for *common time* is ninety steps per minute; for *quick time*, one hundred and ten steps per minute.

The length of the *double step* is thirty-three inches; the cadence is one hundred and sixty-five steps per minute.

The *side step* is six inches.

The *backward step* and *short step* are each fourteen inches, measured from heel to heel.

All steps are executed in quick time unless otherwise specified.

Except in the double step, swinging of the hands or arms should be carefully avoided.

1. *Balance step.* 2. *Left* (or *right*) *foot.* 3. FORWARD. 4. REAR. 5. HALT.

The principles of the direct step are taught thus:

Require the body, shoulders, arms, and hands of the Knights to be kept in *position.* (*Vide* page 12).

At the command *forward*, bend the left knee slightly and carry the left foot, without jerk, about fourteen inches to the front, straightening the knee as the foot is brought forward, the toe turned out and slightly depressed, the sole of the foot about three inches from the ground, the body balanced firmly on the right foot and inclined slightly forward.

At the command *rear*, carry the left foot, without jerk, to the rear, the knee slightly bent, the toe on a line with the heel and inclining slightly downward.

SCHOOL OF THE SELECT KNIGHT.

At the command *halt*, plant the foot by the side of the other. Now exercise with the other foot.

1. *Balance step.* 2. *Left foot.* 3. FORWARD. 4. GROUND. 5. HALT.

At *forward*, advance the left foot as before.

At the command *ground*, plant it without shock, the foot advancing as the weight of the body is brought forward, the left heel twenty-eight inches from the right; the right foot is then advanced to the position of *forward* without command, and similarly planted at the command *ground*.

At the command *halt*, the foot in advance is planted, and the one in rear brought to its side.

Commence at a very slow cadence, afterward increase it gradually to *common time*.

When this is well understood, command:

1. *Forward.* 2. *Common time.* 3. MARCH.

At the command *forward*, throw the weight of the body upon the right leg, without bending the knees.

At the command *march*, move the left foot smartly, but without jerk, twenty-eight inches straight forward, observing carefully the principles explained in the *balance steps;* do not cross the legs or strike one against the other; eyes to the front.

Indicate the cadence by counting *one, two,* etc.

1. *Sir Knights.* 2. HALT.

At the command *halt*, given when either foot is being brought to the ground, bring the foot in rear to its side and plant it without shock.

1. *Forward.* 2. MARCH.

Is the command to march in *quick time* from a halt, always stepping off with the left foot first.

The change to any other cadence is indicated by naming the time before the command *march*, thus: 1. *Common time.* 2.

MARCH; or 1. *Double time.* 2. MARCH; or if at a halt the same commands preceded by *forward*, thus: 1. *Forward.* 2. *Common time.* 3. MARCH, stepping of with the left foot as before.

1. *Short Step.* 2. MARCH.

Being in march; at the second command the length of the step is reduced to fourteen inches without changing the cadence; at the command, 1. *Forward.* 2. MARCH, the full step is resumed.

1. *Mark time.* 2. MARCH.

Being in march; at the second command, given when either foot is coming to the ground, continue the cadence and make a semblance of marching, without gaining ground, by alternately advancing each foot about half its length, the sole parallel with the ground, and bringing it back on a line with the other.

To resume the direct step, the command is: 1. *Forward.* 2. MARCH.

1. *Change step.* 2. MARCH.

At the second command, given the instant either foot strikes the ground, the other foot is advanced and planted; bring the hollow of the foot that is in rear against the heel of the foot in front, and step off promptly with the foot that is in front, carefully keeping up the cadence.

1. *Backward.* 2. MARCH.

Being at a halt, at the second command: Step off with the left foot fourteen inches straight to the rear, measured from heel to heel. At the command, 1. *Sir Knights.* 2. HALT, plant the foot that is in rear and bring the other to its side.

1. *To the rear.* 2. MARCH.

Being in march; at the second command, given as the right foot strikes the ground, advance the left foot to the full step distance and plant it; face to the rear, turning to the

SCHOOL OF THE SELECT KNIGHT. 19

right on the balls of both feet, and immediately step off with the left foot.

    1. *Right* (or *left*) *side step.* 2. MARCH.

At the second command carry the right foot six inches to the right, keeping the knees straight, shoulders square to the front, heels on the same line; plant the right foot and bring the left to its side and so continue, observing the cadence, until halted.

    1. *Double step.* 2. MARCH.

At the first command raise the hands, fingers closed, nails toward the body, left forearm horizontal, elbows to the rear.

At the command *march*, raise the left leg to the front, bending and elevating the knee as much as possible, that part of the leg between the knee and instep vertical, the toe depressed; replace the foot in its former position and execute the same movement with the right leg.

The cadence, one hundred and sixty-five steps per minute, is indicated by the instructor who counts *one, two*, as the feet are successively brought to the ground, commencing in common time and gradually increasing to double time. At the command, 1. *Sir Knights.* 2. HALT, bring back the foot that is raised to the side of the other, and resume the position of a Knight in ranks.

    1. *Forward.* 2. *Double time.* 3. MARCH.

At the first command throw the weight of the body on the right leg; at the second command raise the hands and arms as before explained; at the command *march*, carry forward the left foot, the leg slightly bent, knee somewhat raised, and plant the foot, toe first, thirty-three inches from the right, and so with the right foot, allowing a natural swinging motion of the arms.

Breathe as much as possible through the nose.

To halt, the command is: 1. *Sir Knights.* 2. HALT.

To pass to *quick time*, the command is: 1. *Quick time*

2. MARCH. At the command *march*, plant the foot that is coming to the ground, drop the hands to the side, advance the other foot in *quick time* and plant it twenty-eight inches from the one in rear, resuming or taking up the march in quick time.

    1. *By file.* 2. *Right* (or *left*). 3. DRESS. 4. FRONT.

Place two Knights abreast, two or more yards in advance, to establish the line; at the command *dress*, the others move up, successively, in *quick time*, until about six inches behind the alignment; each then moves on the line, which should never be passed, taking steps of two or three inches, casting the eyes to the right as before explained, keeping the shoulders square to the front, and, without opening his arms, touches with his elbow the Knight on his right.

At the command *front* the habitual position is promptly resumed without jerk.

    1. *Right* (or *left*). 2. DRESS. 3. FRONT.

At the command *dress*, the entire rank, except the Knight established as a basis, moves forward and dresses up to the line as before explained. The instructor verifies the alignment by placing himself about two yards from the right flank facing to the left, orders forward or backward such files as may be in the rear or advance of the line, and commands *front*.

The whole movement should be promptly executed, and no delays be made in alignments.

    1. *Right* (or *left*) *backward.* 2. DRESS. 3. FRONT.

March backward and together until six inches in rear of the line, then dress up, by short steps, as explained.

    1. *Forward.* 2. *Guide right* (or *left*). 3. MARCH.

At the third command, step off smartly with the left foot, the guide marching straight to the front. To do this he must take points in advance perpendicular to the line, and with the greatest care, observe the length and cadence of the steps.

The instructor observes that the Knights touch lightly the elbow toward the side of the guide; that they do not open out either arm; that they yield to pressure coming from the side of the guide and resist pressure coming from the opposite direction; that by shortening or lengthening the steps they gradually recover the alignment and touch of elbow if lost; and that they keep the head and shoulders square to the front; that the guide takes the full step and cadence; that the principles of the step as before explained are carefully observed, in the most minute detail, and that the hands and arms are kept in their proper position, easy and all alike, but without oscillation.

1. *Right* (or *left*). 2. FACE. 3. *Forward.* 4. MARCH.

Being at a halt; face to the right and march as before.

1. *By the right* (or *left*) *flank.* 2. MARCH.

Being in march; the command *march* is given as the right foot strikes the ground; advance and plant the left foot at full distance, then turn to the right and step off in the new direction with the right foot. To march by the *left flank,* apply the general rule, page 11.

In marching in column of files, the Knights cover each other; *keep closed to facing distance,* and avoid spreading the feet and legs apart. Observe that this movement is similar to *right* (or *left*) *face,* except that it is executed in march.

It is habitually executed in *quick time;* but if necessary to march in *double time,* the distance is increased to 21 inches.

1. *Column right* (or *left*). 2. MARCH.

Being in march; at the command *march,* the leading file turns half to the right—that is, at an angle of forty-five degrees—advances one step, and again turning half right, continues the march at right angles with the original direction; thus by two steps describing the arc of a small circle. The other files keep closed up to proper distance and follow in his trace.

1. *Column half right* (or *left*). 2. MARCH.

Is similarly executed.

1. *Forward.* 2. *Column right* (or *left*). 3. MARCH.

Or, 1. *Forward.* 2. *Column half right* (or *left*).
3. MARCH.

Puts a column of files in motion and changes its direction.

1. *Sir Knights.* 2. HALT.

Is the command to halt a column of files; and

1. *Left* (or *right*). 2. FACE.

To face it into line.

1. *By the left* (or *right*) *flank.* 2. MARCH.
3. *Guide left* (or *right*).

Is given when marching in column of files to march in line; or, when marching in line, to march in column of files. In the latter case, omit the third command.

1. *Right* (or *left*) *oblique.* 2. MARCH.

Being in line marching; at the second command each Knight makes a half face to the right and marches straight in the new direction. As they no longer touch elbows, they glance along the shoulders of the nearest files toward the side of the guide, being that to which they are obliqueing, and regulate their steps so that their shoulders are always behind those of the next Knight on that side, and that his head conceals the heads of the others in the rank. The same length of step and same degree of obliquity is preserved, the line of the rank remaining parallel to its original position. Keep the head straight in the direction of the march.

This being a half flank, it is better to give the second command as the right foot strikes the ground, and execute the movement in a manner similar to the *right* (or *left*) *flank*, but it is not deemed absolutely essential.

To resume the originial direction, command, 1. *Forward.* 2. MARCH. The guide is then on the side where it was previous to obliqueing.

If at a halt, the Knights half face to the right at the first command and step off at the command *march.*

If halted while obliqueing, they will halt, pause one cadence of a minute, and face to the front without further command.

The guide is always on the side toward which the oblique is made; on resuming the direct march, the guide is on the side where it was previous to the oblique, without any indication to that effect being given.

In *column of files*, oblique by the same commands and means as when in line, the leading file being the guide.

WHEELINGS

Are of two kinds: on fixed, and on movable pivots.

These are important movements, and each Knight should be required successively to act as pivot, and to conduct the marching flank. The wheeling should also be repeated in double time as soon as the squad is able to execute them properly in quick time.

The fixed pivot—from a halt.

1. *In Circle, right* (or *left*) *wheel.* 2. MARCH.

At the command *march*, all except the pivot, step off with the left foot, at the same time turning the heads a little to the left, the eyes fixed on the eyes of the Knights to the left; the pivot Knight marks time in his place, gradually turning his body to conform to the movement of the marching flank. The one who conducts the marching flank takes steps of twenty-eight inches, and from the first step advances the left shoulder a little, casts his eyes along the rank, and feels lightly the elbow of the next one toward the pivot, but never pushes him. Each of the others lengthen their step in proportion to the distance from the pivot, touches with the elbow toward it and resists pressure from the opposite side, conforms to the movement of the marching flank, and maintains the alignment. After wheeling around the circle several times command, 1. *Sir Knights.* 2. HALT, when all stop and no one stirs. Now point out the defects and mistakes, then command, 1. *Left.* 2. DRESS. 3. FRONT.

1. *Right* (or *left*) *wheel.* 2. MARCH. 3. *Sir Knights.* 4. HALT. 5. *Left* (or *right*). 6. DRESS. 7. FRONT.

Being at a halt; the squad wheels as before on a fixed pivot.

At the fourth command, given when the squad is nearly at right angles with its original position, the line is halted. After pointing out the defects, the instructor immediately dresses the line up to the perpendicular by the fifth and sixth commands; when done, he commands *front*.

To wheel the squad, and move it forward, command:

1. *Right* (or *left*) *wheel*. 2. MARCH. 3. *Forward*. 4. MARCH. 5. *Guide left* (or *right*).

The third command is given in time to add *march* the instant the wheel (one-fourth of a circle) is completed, when they march in the new direction, taking the guide as indicated.

1. *Right* (or *left*) *about*. 2. MARCH. 3. *Sir Knights*. 4. HALT. 5. *Left* (or *right*.) 6. DRESS. 7. FRONT. Or, 3. *Forward*. 4. MARCH. 5. *Guide left* (or *right*).

This wheels the squad in a half circle to the right; when completed the squad is halted or moved forward, as explained before.

Wheeling on a movable pivot.

The wheelings are made by the same commands and means as on a fixed pivot, except that the pivot takes steps of nine inches and thus gains ground forward, describing a small curve so as to clear the wheeling point. The curve is increased in size proportionately with the size of the squad or subdivision, and is equal to about one-half of the front of the squad or subdivision.

The command *forward* is given in time to add *march* the instant the wheel (one-fourth of a circle) is completed, at which all retake the twenty-eight inch step, turn their heads square to the front and march straight forward. The squad may be halted by the same commands and means as before explained.

In wheeling on a movable pivot in double time, the pivot takes steps of eleven inches, and the curve is augmented.

During the wheel the guide is upon the marching flank, and upon completion of the wheel is upon the same flank that it was before the wheel was commenced, without any indication to that effect.

1. *Left* (or *right*) *turn.* 2. MARCH.

Being in march; the first command is given when the rank is three yards from the turning point.

At the command *march*, pronounced the instant the rank is to turn, the Knight on the left, who becomes the guide, faces to the left in marching (that is, executes *by the left flank* in his own person), and moves forward in the new direction without changing the cadence or length of the step. The others advance the shoulders opposite the guide, take the *double time*, and advance in the new direction till they come sucessively on the alignment, then retake the step and cadence from the guide and dress toward him.

In turning in *double time*, those on the side opposite the guide increase the gait in order to come into line.

While this movement should be well learned, the wheel will in nearly all cases effect the desired change of direction.

DOUBLE RANK.

The movements should now be repeated, the Knights being in double rank.

The distance between the ranks is *facing distance;* but on rough ground, or when marching in double time, it is increased to twenty-one inches. Upon halting the rear rank closes, up to facing distance.

In marching in column of files, each rear rank Knight dresses upon his front rank frater, who is the guide of the file.

In changing direction in column of files, each file wheels on a movable pivot.

In obliqueing each rear rank Knight follows the one next on the rank right or left of his front rank frater.

Small legions or less than forty-eight in line, ought not ordinarily to march in double ranks.*

If there is but one Knight in the rear rank of the three on the left of the line, he covers number *one* of the front rank; if there are but two in the rear rank of the left three, they cover numbers *one* and *three* of the front rank.

*A recommendation only.

Manual of the Sword.

Remarks. The rate of swiftness, or time occupied in the execution of each motion, is one-ninetieth of a minute. But in march the cadence of motion is changed to conform to the time indicated by the left foot.

If the sword is grasped too near the guards, or cross, the sword manual is rendered difficult and awkward. Ease and grace of movement in handling the sword can only be acquired by practice, therefore, when the principles and motions are understood, the Knights should frequently practice the manual by themselves. This rule applies as well to the steps, cadence and facings as to the manual.

Avoid the common error of bowing when executing the manual; habitually maintain the erect position.

In *double step*, being at a carry, at the command *double time*, carry the sword straight to the front, the blade vertical, the hand firmly grasping the hilt, the right forearm horizontal, elbow close to the body; if the sword is *at a right shoulder* or *port*, it may so remain, but resume the *carry* after halting, without command, observing the cadence of the step, that is, halt, pause one cadence of the step, then *carry swords*. When part of the leigon executes double time, all execute the manual as if all increased the cadence; on resuming quick time they *carry swords* if so instructed.

In marching, habitually steady the scabbard with the left hadn, fingers next to the leg, thumb to the front.

It is better not to *draw swords* until ranks are formed and to *return* swords before the command *break ranks*.

Substitute *Legions* or *Battalion* for *Sir Knights* when appropriate.

Correctness in detail is of the first importance, therefore each motion should be explained and executed separately, without especial regard to the cadence, until the details are understood. To this end (for example) command; 1. *By the numbers.* 2. *Swords.* 3. PORT. 4. TWO. At the third command the *first motion* of the movement is executed. The instructor corrects the errors, commands *Two*, and the second motion is executed. The rapidity is gradually increased until the cadence is acquired. When the command *by the numbers* is given, it is not repeated, but every succeeding command in the manual is executed with the numbers until the command *without the numbers* is given, or some foot movement intervenes.

The manual should be learned first *by the numbers*, then alternate with and without the numbers, in order to attain the proper cadence and to become proficient in the mechanism.

1. *Draw.* 2. SWORDS.

First motion. At the command *swords*, seize the scabbard near the top, press it against the thigh with the left and grasp the handle with the right hand, at the same time bring the hilt a little forward, and draw the sword until the right forearm is horizontal.

Second motion. Draw the sword quickly, raising the arm to its full extent, at an angle of forty-five degrees upward, in front.

Third motion. Reverse the sword so as to bring it to a *present.* q. v. p. 28.

Fourth motion. Bring the sword-blade vertically back against the right shoulder, edge of the sword to the front, thumb and forefingers embracing the grip, the left side of the grip and the thumb against the thigh, arm nearly extended, the other fingers extended and joined in rear of the grip, elbow near the body; drop the left hand to the side.

Draw.

This is the position of *carry swords.*

If in two ranks, the rear rank takes two backward steps

MANUAL OF THE SWORD.

at the command *draw*, and after executing the fourth motion, pauses one-ninetieth of a minute and steps back to its position.

1. *Present.* 2. SWORDS.

Being at a carry, at the second command bring the sword vertically to the front, raising the hand so that the top of the cross hilt is on a line with the lower part of the chin, and about six inches from it, back of the hand to the front, the right forearm resting along the side and breast, elbow close to the body, helmet of the sword nearly against the breast, the thumb on the back of the grip to the right, the blade inclined to the front at an angle of about sixty-five degrees upward,

Carry.

For officers. At the command *present*, carry the sword to the position just indicated. At the command *swords*, drop the point of the sword near the ground and on a line with the right foot, extending the arm so that the right hand may be brought near to the right thigh, back of the hand to the rear, arm extended, flat of the blade to the front. (This applies to the Commander, Vice and Lieut. Commanders and their superiors only.) It is sometimes referred to as a *salute*, or *officers present*, to distinguish it from *present* of those who are not officers.

Present.

For the standard. (The standard bearer habitually carries the heel of the staff supported at the right hip, the right hand grasping the staff at the height of the shoulder.)

Present.

At the command *present*, slip the right hand along the staff to the height of the eye; at the command *swords*, lower the staff by straightening the arm to its full extent, the heel of the staff remaining at the hip. At *carry swords*, bring back the standard to its habitual place.

Salutes in march by officers and standards are commenced when six yards from the person to be saluted, and cease when six yards past. In saluting, officers turn their heads and look toward the person being saluted simultaneous with the second motion.

Knights in the ranks do not salute, but retain the *carry* when in march.

Salute.

Desiring to cause all to present swords as officers, the command is:

1. *Officers present.* 2. SWORDS.

Which is executed at the second command, as before explained.

1. *Carry.* 2. SWORDS.

From *present*. At the second command bring the sword back to the position of *carry swords*.

Avoid carrying the hand to the front and point of the sword to the rear of the shoulder.

1. *Support.* 2. SWORDS.

First motion. Bring the sword vertically to the front of the center of the body, the cross nearly as high as the breast, and six inches from it.

Support.

Second motion. Carry the sword to the left side, guards opposite the hollow of the elbow, bring the left hand up and grasp the right elbow, thumb over and resting on the right forearm, the cross (guard) resting on the left arm near the elbow, left forearm over the right, blade perpendicular.

MANUAL OF THE SWORD.

1. *Carry.* 2. SWORDS.

Swords Port.

First motion. Seize the blade, without deranging its position, with the thumb and forefingers of the left hand, left elbow close to the body, as a pivot.

Second motion. Carry the sword vertically with both hands to its place at *carry*, fingers extended and joined, pressing the sword gently against the hollow of the shoulder, back of the hand to the front and at the height of the shoulder, elbow near the body.

Third motion. Drop the left hand to the side.

1. *Swords.* 2. PORT.

First motion. Seize the blade at the shoulder with the left hand. *Second motion.* Bring the sword diagonally across the front of the body, flat of the blade to the front and resting in the left hand at the height of the breast, thumb extended in rear along the blade toward the point, the right hand grasping the hilt and nearly in front of the right hip, edge of the sword down.

1. *Carry.* 2. SWORDS.

First motion. Bring back the sword with both hands, the left hand as high as the right arm-pit, pressing the blade to its place, fingers extended at the height of the shoulder, elbow near the body, back of hand to the front.

Second motion. Drop the left hand to the side.

1. *Order.* 2. SWORDS.

Drop the sword-point to the ground, about an inch from the point of the right toe and on line with the toes; sword vertical, the right hand resting on the helmet, back of the hand up, first three fingers in front touching the grip, the thumb and little finger partially embracing it.

Order.

MANUAL OF THE SWORD. 31

1. *Carry*. 2. SWORDS.

Bring the sword back to its position in *carry*.

1. *With sword*. 2. CHARGE.

Execute the first motion of *about face* (*vide* page 15), except that the right heel is in rear of the left; bend the left knee a little, inclining the body forward, the weight principally on the left foot, at the same time drop the point of the sword forward to the height of the belt, the right hand firmly grasping the handle, thumb against the hip. (This can also be executed in march, the shoulders being kept square to the front.)

1. *Carry*. 2. SWORDS.

Charge.

Face to the front, resuming the position of *carry swords*.

1. *Right shoulder*. 2. SWORDS.

Bring the flat of the sword upon the right shoulder, guard as high as the arm-pit, thumb nearly touching the side of the right breast, point of the sword up to the left and rear so as to clear the chapeau.

1. *Carry*. 2. SWORDS.

Resume that position.

1. *Support*. 2. SWORDS.

The sword being at a *right shoulder*. *First motion*. Lower the sword and bring it to the center of the body, to the position of the first motion of *support swords* from a *carry*.

Second motion. Carry it to the left side as before explained. (*Vide* page 29.)

1. *Carry*. SWORDS.

(*Vide* explanation, p. 30, after *support swords*.)

Right Shoulder.

1. *Rear rest.* 2. Swords.

First motion. Execute the *right shoulder swords*, as explained.

Second motion. Drop the sword-point to the left and rear and let the blade rest across the shoulders in rear of the neck, at the same time raise the left hand, palm to the front, and grasp the blade near the shoulder with the fingers and thumb, holding the grip in like manner with the fingers and thumb of the right hand, elbows close to the body. Care should be taken not to derange the position of the head and shoulders in executing this movement.

Rear rest Swords.

1. *Carry.* 2. Swords.

First motion. Drop the left hand to the side and come to the position of *right shoulder swords*.

Second motion. Resume the carry.

1. *Reverse.* 2. Swords.

First motion. Raise and carry the sword vertically to the front, the elbow advanced and forming an obtuse angle.

Second motion. Bring the point down to the front and rear, turning the sword by a wrist movement completely around, so that the edge will be down and the blade inclined to the rear forty-five degrees downward; at the same time carry the left forearm horizontally behind the back, the left hand, palm out, clasping the blade; support the sword with the elbow against the right side, assisted by the left hand in rear, holding the grip with the thumb and forefinger of the right hand, the other fingers successively more curved, the guards (cross) nearly against the shoulder.

1st motion, Reverse.

1. *Carry.* 2. SWORDS.

First motion. Retake the first position of *reverse* by inverse means.

Second motion. Resume the carry.

1. *Sword-arm.* 2. REST.

Bring the right hand in front of the body, arm extended, blade resting along the right forearm and diagonally across the body; embrace the back of the right hand with the fingers and palm of the left. Resume the carry at the command.

1. *Parade.* 2. REST.

Reverse.

First motion. Carry the right foot three inches to the rear, the left knee slightly bent, resting the weight of the body principally on the right foot. *Second motion.* Drop the sword-point to the ground, to the right and on a line with the great toe of the left foot, parallel to the front; the sword vertical, in front of the center of the body; fingers and thumb holding the helmet, which rests in the palm of the right hand, back of the hand up, embraced and covered by the left hand.

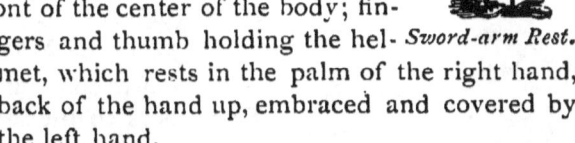
Sword-arm Rest.

Being at parade rest: 1. *Rest on.* 2. SWORDS.

Incline the head to the front. At the command *Sir Knight*, raise the head. (See page 35.)

1. *Sir Knights* (or *Legion*). 2. ATTENTION.

3. *Carry.* 4. SWORDS.

At the second command bring the right foot to the side of the left, body erect, in position; drop the left hand to the side, the right hand hanging naturally at the side and holding the grip,

Parade Rest. sword-blade inclining across and in front of right

leg, the sword-point undisturbed. At the fourth command bring the sword to a carry.

1. *From right open files.* 2. MARCH.

At the first command, all, except the Knight on the right, who stands at a carry, turn the head and drop the sword-point to the right, hand at right breast, sword horizontal. At the command *march*, they take the left side-step, all stepping together, until each in succession has gained such interval that the sword-point will touch the left arm of the Knight on the right, observing that the alignment is preserved; as each gains this interval, he turns the head to the front and resumes the carry.

From right open files.

1. *From left open files.* 2. MARCH.

Is similarly executed, except that the right hand is at the breast, guards in front of the left arm, the sword horizontal to the left in prolongation of the right forearm.

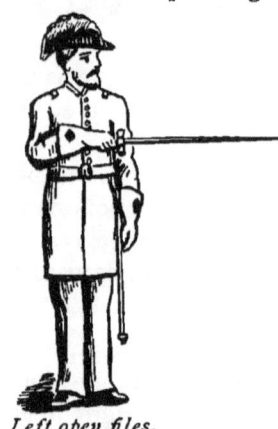

Left open files.

1. *Right* (or *left*). 2. FACE. 3. *Close files.* 4. MARCH.

At the fourth command the Knight in front faces to the left; the others close up in quick time and successively face to the left, dress to the right, and immediately turn the head to the front.

1. *Cross.* 2. SWORDS.

The lines being fully two yards apart and facing each other.

First motion. Bring the sword to a *present*. *Second motion.* Plant the right foot sixteen inches straight to the front, right knee slightly bent, at same time raising right hand, arm extended wrist as high as the head, sword in prolongation of the arm, thumb extended along the left of the grip, back of sword up; cross the swords six inches from their points with the Knight opposite, at the same instant plant the foot with very light shock.

1 Carry. 2 Swords.

Cross Swords.

First motion. Bring back the foot to its former place and the sword to a *present*. *Second motion.* Resume the *carry*.

1. *Sir Knights.* 2. Kneel.

Being at *parade rest*.

First motion. Carry the right foot about twenty-eight inches to the rear.

Second motion. Kneel on the right knee so that its front and rear of the left heel will be on a line parallel with the front; head erect.

1. *Rest on.* 2. Swords.

Incline the head to the front.

1. *Sir Knights.* 2. Rise.

At the first command, raise the head. At the second command, rise. *Second motion.* Bring the right foot near to the left, resuming the position of *parade rest*.

Kneeling, rest on.

MANUAL OF THE SWORD.

1. *Sir Knights.* 2. ATTENTION. 3. *Carry.* 4. SWORDS.

Resume that position.

1. *Sir Knights.* 2. *Return.* 3. SWORDS.

At the command *return*, sieze the scabbard with the left hand, near the top, inclining it a little forward, and bring the sword about six inches in front of the left shoulder, blade vertical, lower part of the hand at the height of the chin. *Second motion.* Lower the blade across and along the left arm, the point to the rear; turn the head slightly to the left, fixing the eyes on the opening of the scabbard, and insert the blade, assisted by the thumb and forefinger of the left hand, until the right forearm is horizontal. At the command *swords*, return the blade, turn the head to the front and drop the hands to the sides. (The second motion should occupy the time of three motions.) If in two ranks, at the command *return*, the rear rank takes two backward steps, and resumes its place, after the execution of the command *swords.*

Return.

1. *Secure.* 2. SWORDS.

The sword being in the scabbard.

First motion. At the command *swords*, seize the scabbard with the left hand, palm front, thumb to the left, arm extended. *Second motion.* Raise the sword (in the scabbard), bring the left hand in front and nearly as high as the belt and a little to the left of the buckle, the sword (in the scabbard), resting along the left forearm, back of the hand down, the cross at the hollow of the elbow.

1. *Drop.* 2. SWORDS.

Lower the sword (in the scabbard) to its place.

Secure.

1. *Inspection.* 2. SWORDS.

First motion. Come to a *present.*

Second motion. Turn the wrist outward to show the other side of the blade, pause slightly, and turn the wrist back.

Third motion. Resume the carry.

[Executed successively as inspector approaches.]

For the Chapeau or Cap.

1. *Sir Knights.* 2. UN-COVER.*

First motion. Take the chapeau (or cap) by the front piece with the left hand. *Second motion.* Raise the chapeau and place it on the right shoulder, slightly inclined to the front, holding it in that position with the left hand.

1. *Sir Knights.* 2. RE-COVER.*

First motion. Replace the chapeau (or cap) on the head.

Second motion. Drop the hand to the side.

Never execute the *uncover* unless the swords are sheathed, at an *order,* or (with the right hand) when at a *secure.*

Uncover.

To *uncover and present at the same time is unmilitary and awkward.*

The *uncover* may be executed by signals, thus:

First motion. Extend the left hand in front of the breast, palm up, fingers extended and joined. *Second motion.* Execute the first motion of *uncover.* *Third motion.* Execute the second motion of *uncover.*

To recover by signals. *First motion.* Slowly raise the chapeau from the shoulder and place it on the head. *Second motion.* Drop the hand to the side.

---

*Dwell slightly on the first syllable.

THE SILENT MANUAL.

When the foregoing has been well learned it may be executed, being at "open order" (*vide* School of the Legion) at the commands:

1. *Continue the manual.* 2. *Present.* 3. SWORDS.

At the command *swords*, the manual is executed in the following order, without pause, except that the regular cadence of motion is preserved throughout.

1. Present, swords. 2. Carry, swords.
3. Officers present, swords. 4. " "
5. Support, swords. 6. " "
7. Swords, port. 8. " "
9. Order, swords. 10. " "
11. With swords, charge. 12. " "
13. Right shoulder, swords. 14. " "
15. Right shoulder, swords.
16. Support, swords. 17. " "
18. Rear rest, swords. 16. " "
20. Reverse, swords. 21. " "
22. Sword-arm, rest. 23. " "
24. Front rank, about, face. The rear rank files (by one side-step about eighteen inches to the right, if it be single rank open order) cover the files in the front rank simultaneously with their *about face.*
25. Cross, swords. 26. Carry, swords.
27. Front rank, about, face. Rear rank recovers intervals, by a side step to the left, at same instant with the *about face* of the front rank.
28. Parade rest.
29. Sir Knights, kneel. 30. Rest on, swords.
31. Sir Knights, rise. 32. Sir Knights, attention.
33. Carry, swords. 34. Return, swords.
35. Secure, swords. 36. Drop, swords.
37. Sir Knights, un-cover. 38. Sir Knights, re-cover.
39. Right hand, salute. 40. Left hand, salute.
41. Draw, swords. 42. Parade, rest.

The *open files* is omitted.

The whole of the *silent manual* occupies eighty-ninetieths of a minute, including the command.

Or 80 seconds if seconds be the cadence. A pause of one cadence may be made between each completed sword movement, if so instructed.

The Vice and Lieut. Commanders stand at *order swŏrds* during silent manual, unless otherwise instructed.

THE SALUTES.

When addressed, face the Knight challenging the inferior in rank, then, if the swords are drawn, salutes with it; this is acknowledged, and both resume the *carry* simultaneously, or the junior may stand at a *present* while making a short report.

If swords are not drawn, the inferior in rank gives the *first motion* of the hand-salute, which is acknowleged in full; the inferior in rank executes the *second* and *third motions,* so that the hands of both Knights may be dropped to the side at the same instant. The sword is never drawn to acknowledge a salute already given.

If the ∴ C ∴ is sitting, he salutes with the hand, although his sword may be drawn. He does not rise to acknowledge salutes of an inferior in rank, but inferiors when in the Lodge room or in uniform, if not engaged in some particular duties, arise when addressed by official superiors.

In passing a Knight, salute with hand farthest from him, turn the head toward him, simultaneous with the second motion, looking the person saluted steadily in the face.

An officer or Knight mounted, dismounts before addressing official superiors not mounted.

School of the Officers.

Theory and practice should go hand in hand. Officers should be competent to take command in the absence of official superiors, and every one be able to command his subdivision with credit. A careless or ill-informed officer may cause the best drilled legion to appear at great disadvantage or throw it into confusion. An indolent manner of giving commands is demoralizing in its tendency; hence subordinates should be practiced in squad or platoon drills as chiefs, that they may become familiar with their duties and energetic and prompt, requiring every Knight to be equally prompt and attentive.

The idea that discipline cannot be maintained among Select Knights is sheer nonsense, yet the instructor need not forget that his men are gentlemen, who, out of ranks, are his peers.

An *officer's squad* should be organized, admitting as supernumeraries Knights who will take an interest in it and fill the places of absentees. Its members should be six or twelve besides the chief. Every member should be faithful and prompt in attendance, cheerfully obedient to orders, attentive and silent in ranks.

The chief of the Select Knights, when in command, temporarily or otherwise, must have absolute control. He indicates the lessons to be learned, commencing with the vocabulary, and proceeds regularly through without omitting anything. One of the most important requisites is promptness; therefore having announced the lesson and hour for meeting, the chief should himself be ready, and, before the clock ceases to strike, command: FALL IN. He should always be prompt in time, prompt in giving and obeying orders, and prompt in the "etiquette of Knightly courtesy." Promptly meet, promptly commence and promptly dismiss the squad.

After the oral lesson the squad should be drilled in it well and thoroughly; or, better, as each motion is explained by a Knight, require its execution, until the principles are well understood.

Take frequent rests of two or three minutes only, when discussion may be indulged in; but at the command *attention* conversation stops instanter. Discussion while under instruction should not be permitted; then the chief's *ipse dixit* is law final.

Perfect discipline should be observed from the first. It is quite as proper to talk during the conference of the degrees as to talk during drill.

The officers should alternate in exercising the squad in the drill, under supervision of the chief, whose criticisms should be for the benefit of all, not prosy but clear and pointed explanations, without circumlocution or unnecessary comment.

The instructor ought never to require a movement to be made until he has fully explained it, and sees that *no movement, however trivial it may appear, is performed carelessly or with undue haste* He should practice the officers and guides, especially in estimating distances and in becoming familiar with the bugle and sword signals. The *assembly, forward, halt* and *threes right* are particularly important when Select Knights assemble in large numbers.

By giving each frequent opportunities to command, errors may be corrected, uniformity secured, ambition to excel stimulated, closer attention and study encouraged and the general interest increased.

All commands to Knights, under arms, are given with the sword drawn. If for any purpose Select Knights or other orders or troops are together, officers execute the first motion of *officers present* at the command *present*, and the second motion at the command *arms* (or *saber*) and the Knights *present swords*. In like manner, at the command *fours right* (or *left*) *march*, Select Knights execute *threes right* (or *left*) *march*. At the command *Platoons right wheel*, etc., Select Knights execute *Divisions* (or *double sections*) *right wheel*, and so on. At the command, *parade rest*, the Lieut. Commanders and officers of higher rank (not giving the order) take that position; at the command *attention*, they *carry swords*.

When marching in double time, officers who are in command, so that their position is in front or a yard or more from the flank, bring their swords to the position of *port*, steadying the scabbards with the left hand.

About face for officers. At the command *about*, carry the toe of the right foot about eight inches to the rear and three inches to the left of the left heel, without deranging the direction of the left foot. At the command *face*, turn to the right, upon the left heel and right toe, face to the rear and replace the right heel by the side of the left.

If so directed, officers omit the manual, except the *present*, *order, parade rest, rest on swords*, and *uncover*

THE BAND.

The Drum-major faces the band and gives the signal to march. His position is two yards in front of the center of the band.

The counter-march is executed by the file leaders to the right of the Drum-major, wheeling individudally about to the right, those to his left to the left; the other men of each file follow their file leaders. The Drum-major passes through the center.

In executing *rear open order*, each rank of the band steps back three yards from the rank in its front, the front being on a line with the front rank of the legion and six yards from its right.

Bands should be required to keep their proper distances and

take the full twenty-eight inch step, also that they should be careful to keep the time with each other, when practicable; and, if near together, two should not play at the same time.

At the command *halt*, the music ceases.

Do not take it for granted that the band is familiar with the cadence in *common* and *quick time,* but test its accuracy by the watch and notice the length of its step.

School of the Legion.

Remarks. Thorough instruction in the elementary School of the Knight is absolutely essential to success in the movements of the legion, which depend upon the precision of the drill. This can only be attained by *practice, the strictest attention of every Knight*, and the intelligent assistance of the chiefs of subdivisions. One awkward Knight, or the swinging of a single hand, will wholly destroy the beauty of the line.

In this work "file closers" have been dispensed with, and officers are assigned places that will utlize every available uniform in extending the lines, because many legions are small, and compartively few of their members are equipped; hence they can ill afford to scatter their numerical strength; and because the necessity for file closers does not appear in the movements of a Legion, as is claimed for the operations of belligerents, nor do they add to the symmetry of the formations for display.

The Past Officers wearing shoulder-straps form on the right according to height, but have no other distinction.

The Commander as instructor goes wherever his presence is necessary; in column his place is on the left of the Vice-Commander, or four yards to the left and abreast of the leading subdivision; if the Legion be in line, his post is two yards in front of the center, or on the right flank at the right of the Vice-Commander. (See p. 11.)

The Vice-Commander in line is on the right flank; in column of divisions, as chief of the first division, he marches two yards in front of its center. He is also the right or left guide,

SCHOOL OF THE LEGION. 45

according as in the maneuvers he finds himself on the right or left of the Legion.

The Lieut.-Commander in line, is in like manner on the left flank as *left guide*. He is chief of the rear division when the right is in front, and of the leading division when the left is in front.

It is the duty of the Vice. and Lieut.-Commanders to assist the Commander in maintaining order in the ranks, habitually preserving their own correct position, and, if necessary, they caution the Knightst in a low tone.

The Senior Workman, Standard Bearer and Junior Workman form as the *Standard Guard*.

The Senior Workman is on the right, and the Junior Workman on the left, of the Standard Bearer. These three form the Standard Guard, whose place is in the front rank and as near the center of the Leigon as practicable.

A Leigon is divided into two, and, if desirable, into three or four (nearly) equal parts; each part is called a *division*, the odd number of threes, being in the division on the left. It is better that there should be but two divisions, so designated when the Legion is formed. But for the purpose of placing the Standard in a center division, there may be three, or in order to equally divide the Legion into four parts, to form square. when double sections will not acomplish it, four division may be formed. In line of three ranks the front rank is the *first division*, the middle rank the *second division*, and the rear rank the *third division*. In column, the leading vision is the *first division*, whether the right or the left is in front.

The chief of a subdivision is the officer or Knight on its right, unless otherwise specially designated.

The guide of a subdivision is generally the Knight on its left. Subdivisions are designated numerically from the right to left, when in line, and from the head of the column to the rear. The designation changes when by facing, etc., the left becomes the right; officers in command caution *first division*, etc., whenever the designation is changed.

FORMATION OF A LEGION.

At the sound of the *assembly* every Knight hastens to the place from which the sound came, *promptness* being the first most excellent quality for a well drilled Legion.

The Vice-Commander commands:

FALL IN.

and indicates the basis for the line by placing the tallest Knight upon it; he then places himself six yards in front of the center, facing it.

The Knights form in column of files faced to right, graduated in height from front to rear, tallest in front, swords at *carry*. (See p. 26.)

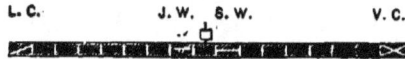

The Vice-Commander now commands:

Forward. 2. *Guide right (or left).* 3. MARCH.

1. *Left.* 2. FACE. 3. COUNT THREES.

The Knights on the right (front and rear rank) counts *one*, the next at his left says *two*, the next *three*, the next *one*, and so on to the left, without turning their heads, but counting in a firm, quick tone. Observing the cadence adds much to the appearance and effect.

(The Vice-Commander in his own person may act as number one in leading three in small Legions, and the Lieut.-Commander may march with the left three if the number is wanting.)

The Vice-Commander then commands: ONES COUNT, when numbers one of each three sucessively turn their heads to the left, at the same time count *one*, *two*, etc., from right to left, and immediately turn the head to the front. The odd threes are the right and the even threes the left of sections. He then indicates the right and left of divisions, leaving the odd three in the left division, and commands:

1. *Second Division.* 2. *Left side step.* 3. MARCH. 4. *Division.* 5. HALT.

The fifth command is given when the division has gained an interval of two yards.

In the meantime, the Standard Guard (with the standard) forms six yards from the left, perpendicular to the line, and in inverse order; that is, the Recorder is on the left and the Treasurer on the right of the Standard Bearer.

The Vice-Commander now commands.

1. *Standard Guard.* 2. POST. 3. *Present.* 4. SWORDS.

The line *presents* and guard marches, under direction of the Sen.Work. standard saluting, between the Legion and Vice-Commander, opposite to its place, wheels to the right, marches through the opening between the divisions and halts, comes to an *about face*, and the Vice-Commander immediately commands:

1. *Carry.* 2. SWORDS. 3. *Right.* 4. DRESS. 5. FRONT. 6. *Present.* 7. SWORDS.

This is acknowledged by the Commander, who raises his chapeau, he having taken position three yards in rear of the Vice-Commander and facing the Legion. He stands with arms folded until just before the command to *present.*

The Vice-Commander comes to an *about face*, salutes with the sword, and says:,

Sir, the Legion is formed.

The salute is acknowledged with the hand, and the Commander orders:

Take your post, Sir Knight.

The Vice-Commander faces about, marches to within one yard of the line, turns to the left, and, when opposite his place, turns to the right and halts in rear of it, faces about and dresses on the line.

When he faces the Legion to the left into line (if so instructed) he brings it to *support swords* and calls the roll, each Knight answers *Here* when his name is called, and brings his sword to a *carry* then to an *order*.

This is the formal ceremony, but the Commander may, in emergencies, order the Legions to *fall in*, *left face*, *count threes*, *ones count*, and designate the division only.

To Form in two Ranks.

The Knights *fall in* as explained; the commander orders:

1, *In two ranks form Legion.* 2. MARCH.

At the second command the Vice-Commander and the Knight on the right face to the left (front). The second Knight places himself in rear, covering the first one, the others close in quick time, form alternately in the front and rear rank, and each faces to the front upon arriving in his proper place; then *count threes* as before explained. Or, the Knights may fall in, if so instructed, in two ranks, faced to the right, and the formation is completed as before.

To Dismiss the Legion.

Being in line at a halt.

1. *Return.* 2. SWORDS. 3. *Break ranks.* 4. MARCH.

To Open Ranks.

Being at a halt.

1. *Rear open order.* 2. MARCH. 3. FRONT.

At the first command the Vice and Lieut.-Commanders march backward three yards to mark the new alignment. At the comand *march* the front rank dresses to the right, the rear rank casts the eyes to the right and steps backward, halts a little in rear of the alignment and dresses to the right on the line established by the Vice and Lieut.-Commanders. The Commander verifies the alignment of the front and the Vice-Commander of the rear rank. At the command *front*, the Vice and Lieut.-Commanders place themselves three yards in front of the center of their divisions.

SCHOOL OF THE LEGION.

1. *Close order.* 2. MARCH.

At the command *march*, the officers face about, approach to within one yard of the line, march along its front, and resume their place in line, the rear rank closes up in quick time to facing distance, each Knight covering his front rank frater.

In Line, Single Rank, to Open Order.

The same rules and commands apply as in double ranks, except that *twos* are counted, if not otherwise known (see Display Drill); the even numbers march straight backward and form the rear rank, in open order, so as to be exactly in rear of their own intervals between numbers *one* of the front rank. When ranks are closed, they resume their places in line.

To March in Line.

1. *Forward.* 2. *Guide right* (or *left*). 3. MARCH.

At the command *march*, all step off with the left foot, in quick time, the Vice-Commander as right guide taking points in advance perpendicular to the line, and with the greatest care observes the length and cadence of the steps. The touch of the elbow toward the guide is kept up, and the alignment carefully preserved. This should be frequently practiced, and for long distances.

1. *Legion.* 2. HALT.

At the second command every Knight halts, and the alignment is made.

To Wheel the Legion.

Being in line at a halt.

1. *Right* (or *left*) *wheel.* 2. MARCH. 3. *Legion*, 4. HALT. 5. *Left* (or *right*). 6. DRESS. 7. FRONT.

At the command *march*, the Legion wheels to the right on a fixed pivot. The Vice-Commander stands fast, so that the breast of the pivot Knight may rest against his left arm at the completion of the wheel. The Commander superintends the wheel, moves backward by the shortest line to a point

Legion, distance where the left of the line will rest, directly in front of the Vice-Commander, and facing him. At the command *halt*, given when the left guide is three yards from the perpendicular, the Legion halts, and the Lieut.-Commander promptly places himself so that his breast will touch the Commander's right arm, who steps back two yards and commands *left*, DRESS, when the Knights dress up to the line of the pivot and Lieut.-Commander. At the command *front* the Vice-Commander places himself in line on the right of the pivot.

To *continue the march* upon completion of the wheel, the Commander orders *forward*, when the Lieut.-Commander arrives at three yards from the perpendicular, adding MARCH the instant the wheel is completed, and *guide left* (or *right*) immediately afterward. At the command *forward* the Vice-Commander places himself at the side of the pivot.

In all wheels the guide is on the marching flank, and slightly advances the shoulder opposite the pivot, keeping the pivot constantly in view.

In wheeling on a movable pivot, the command *forward* is given in time to add *march* the instant the wheel is completed, and the guide is announced on either flank.

To *continue the wheel*, that caution is given as the marching flank approaches the perpendicular, and the wheeling is kept up as if but just commenced. If on a fixed pivot, the guide on the pivot flank places himself in line at the side of the pivot Knight, and halts as before. This may be continued *ad libitum*, or the direction of the wheel may be changed at the command: 1. *Left* (or *right*) *wheel*. 2. MARCH, when the same principle will govern as before.

To Effect a Slight Change of Direction.

Incline to the right (or *left*): Is given in march.

The guide avdances gradually the left shoulder and marches in the new direction; all the files advance the left shoulder and conform to the movements of the guide, lengthening or

SCHOOL OF THE LEGION. 51

shortening the step according as the change is toward the side of the guide or the side opposite.

While this should be learned a half wheel will ordinarily effect the desired object.

To Turn.

1. *Right* (or *left*) *turn.* 2. MARCH,

Is given when marching in line.

At the second command the Vice-Commander faces to the right, without halting, and continues the march; all the files increase the gait and hasten to his left, taking the step and touch of elbow from him on arriving in line.

Right (or *left*) *half turn* is similarly executed.

To March by the Flank.

Being in line at a halt.

1. *Right* (or *left*). 2. FACE. 3. *Forward.* 4. MARCH.

Or, 1. *By the right* (or *left*) *flank.* 2. MARCH, if in march,

Or, from a halt or in march command:

1. *Threes right* (or *left*). 2. MARCH.

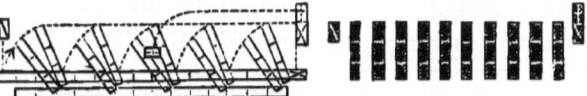

At the command *march*, each three wheels to the right on a fixed pivot. Upon completion of the wheel the front rank of each three takes the full step, the rear ranks fall back until there are twenty-one inches between the front and rear ranks. The front rank of the second three will be twenty-one inches from the rear rank of the first three, and so on to the rear of the column.

The Vice and Lieut.-Commanders each march forty-four inches to the front and face to the right; the Vice-Commander places himself twenty-one inches in front of the left file of the first three, and marches on a line parallel to the former front of the Legion, and the Lieut.-Commander follows twenty-one inches in rear of the left file of the last three. This brings the front rank of each three at wheeling distance, as they would be, had there been but one rank in the line; the rear ranks are half way between the front ranks of the threes.

In wheeling by threes the *forward march* is always taken up on completion of the wheel unless, the command *halt* is given.

To March in Column of Threes to the Front.

Being in line, the Commander orders:

1. *Right* (or *left*) *forward*. 2. *Threes right* (or *left*).
3. MARCH.

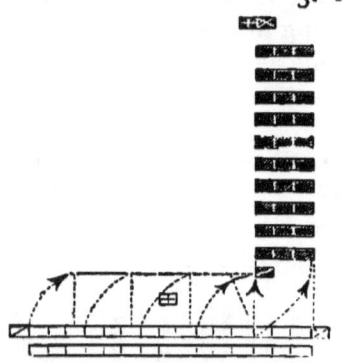

At the third command the Vice-Commander places himself in front of the left file of the right three, the right three moves straight to the front, shortening the first three steps; the rear rank, if there be one, falls back to half distance, the other threes wheel to the right on a fixed pivot; the second three, when its wheel is two-thirds completed, wheels to the left on the left on a movable pivot and follows the first three, and the others, having wheeled to the right, move forward and wheel to the left on the same ground as the second.

To Change Direction of Column.

Being in march.

1. *Column right* (or *left*). 2. MARCH.

If the change of direction be to the side opposite the guide, he wheels as if on the marching flank of a rank of three; if the change of direction be toward the side of the guide, he shortens his step at the command *march* and wheels; the leading three wheels on a movable pivot, its pivot following the trace of the guide. The wheel being completed, the guide and leading rank retake the twenty-eight inch step; the other threes move forward and wheel on the same ground.

SCHOOL OF THE LEGION.

1. *Column half right* (or *left*). 2. MARCH. Is similarly executed.

1. *Forward.* 2. *Column right* (or *left*). 3. MARCH.

Or, 1. *Threes right.* 2. *Column right.* 3. MARCH.

puts the column in motion and changes the step at the same time.

To Halt a Column and put it in Motion.

1. *Legion.* 2. HALT. Or, 1. *Forward.* 2. MARCH.

To Oblique in Column.

In obliqueing in column of threes or subdivision, the guide, without indication, is always on the side toward which the oblique is made. On resuming the direct march the guide, without indication, is on the same side it was previous to the oblique.

Practice obliqueing in column and in line often and for a long distance at a time, that the errors may be seen and corrected.

1. *Right* (or *left*) *oblique.* 2. MARCH.

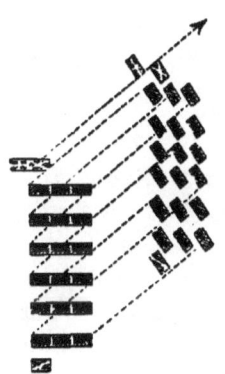

During the oblique the threes preserve their parallelism; the Knight in each rank of threes on the side toward which the oblique is made is the guide of the rank. The leading guide is the guide of the column when the oblique is toward his flank. If toward the opposite flank the guide of the front rank of the leading three is the guide of the column.

1. *Forward.* 2. MARCH.

Is given to resume the direct march.

To March a Column of Threes to the Rear.

1. *Threes right* (or *left*) *about.* 2. MARCH.

Each rank of three wheels about on a fixed pivot and marches to the former rear. The rear ranks, if there are two ranks, preserve their distances of twenty-one inches from the front ranks when in column of threes; the pivot of the rear rank closes up to his front rank pivot, covers him during the wheel and, on its completion, falls back to twenty-one inches.

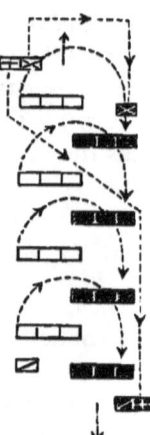

The guide at the head of the column takes two steps forward, faces to the right, and places himself, on completion of the about, in rear of the file on the marching flank of the now rear three. The guide at the rear of the column faces to the right and places himself, on completion of the about, in front of the file on the marching flank of the now leading three.

The Commander faces about and hastens to place himself on the left of the guide at the head of the column.

If the movement is made to the left, the leading guide takes two steps straight forward and faces about; the leading three wheels past him, when he places himself twenty-one inches in rear of its left file by retracing his steps; the guide in rear of the column faces about and preserves his distance, marching forward when the movement is completed.

To Form Line from Column of Threes.

1. *Threes right* (or *left*). 2. MARCH. 3. *Guide right* (or *left*). Or, 3. *Legion*. 4. HALT. 5. *Left* (or *right*.) 6. DRESS. 7. FRONT.

The threes wheel to the right into line on a fixed pivot.

If in two ranks, the rear rank closes to facing distance during the wheel, and if executed in *double time*, regains the distance of twenty-one inches. Should the line advance when formed, the guide, if in front of the pivot, takes two steps forward and faces to the right, placing himself on the left of the leading three upon completion of the wheel. If in front of the marching flank, he wheels to the right with the leading three, obliqueing at the same time so as to uncover the file, and places himself on the left of the file when the wheel is completed. The guide in rear takes his place on the right of the Legion, and the guide is announced the instant the threes unite in line.

If the command *halt* be given as the threes wheel into line, the Commander places the leading guide on the line of the pivots at sufficient distance to admit the leading three which dresses on the guide; the others dress up to the pivot of the three in front, thus insuring a prompt alignment.

1. *On right* (or *left*) *into line*. 2. March. 3. *Legion*. 4. Halt. 5. *Right* (or *left*). 6. Dress. 7. Front.

At the command *march*, the leading three wheels to the right on a movable pivot, and moves forward, dressing on the guide, who places himself on its right and conducts it. The other threes march a distance equal to their fronts, beyond the wheeling point of the three next preceding, wheel to the right and advance, as did the first three. The rear guide places himself on the left of the rear three as it wheels to the right.

At the command *halt*, given when the leading three has advanced Legion distance in the new direction, or at a less distance if desired by the Commander, it halts, and at the

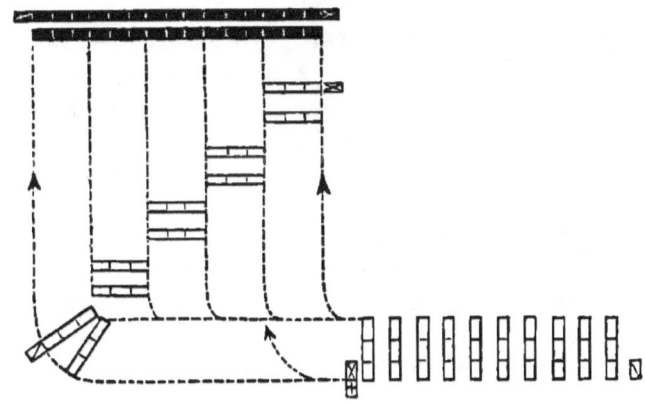

sixth command, given immediately after, dresses to the right. The other threes halt and dress successively on arriving in line. The rear rank, if there is one, closes to facing distance upon halting.

The seventh command is given when the last three has dressed.

If in double rank, and it is desired to form line in single rank, precede the first command by, 1. *In single rank*. 2. *On right into line*, etc., and the rear ranks execute the movement the same as the others, passing a distance equal to their front beyond where their front ranks wheeled.

If in single rank, to *form in double rank*, the command is, 1. *In double rank*. 2. *On right into line*, etc. The movement is similar. The rear rank of each three wheels to the right on the same ground as its front rank.

If marching in double time, or in *quick time*, and the command be *double time*, the Select Commander orders *guide right* when the leading three has wheeled out of the column; it then advances in quick time; the others continue the double time until they successively arrive in line, when they take the step and alignment from the guide.

Front into Line in Single and Double Rank.

1. *Right* (or *left*) *front into line*. 2. MARCH. 3. *Legion*. 4. HALT. 5. *Left* (or) *right*. 6. DRESS. 7. FRONT.

At the second command the first three moves straight to the front, dressing on the leading guide, who places himself on its left; the other threes oblique to the right till opposite their places in line, when each in succession marches forward.

At the command *halt*, given when the leading three has advanced legion distance, it halts, and at the sixth command, given immediately after, dresses to the left. The other threes halt and dress to the left upon arriving in line. The rear ranks close to facing distance upon halting. The guide in rear places himself on the right of the front rank

SCHOOL OF THE LEGION.

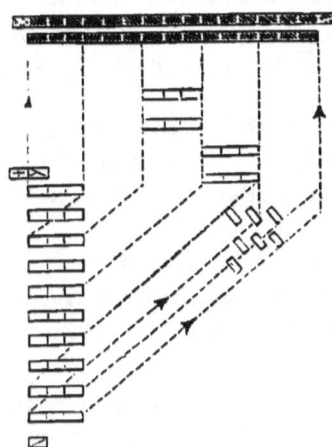

when the last three arrives in line.

If marching in double time, or in *quick time,* and the command is *double time,* the Commander orders *guide left* immediately after the command *march;* the leading three advance in quick time, the others oblique in double time; each resumes the forward march when opposite its place, taking the step and alignment from the guide (or dresses) as it arrives in line.

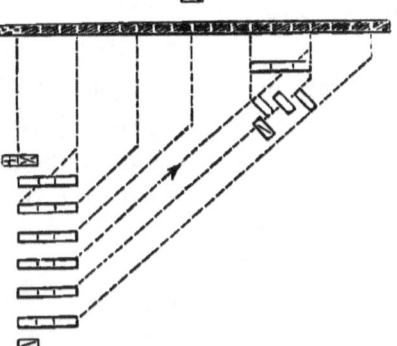

If in double rank, and it is desired to form in single rank, the command is, 1. *In single rank.* 2. *Right* (or *left*) *front into line,* etc. Each rear line obliques until it has gained a distance equal to its front beyond the point where their front rank commenced the forward, which is opposite their place in line, when they too march to the front, halting and dressing as explained.

If in single rank, to form in double rank in line, the principles are the same; the command will then be, 1. *In double rank.* 2. *Right front into line,* etc. The rear rank of each three obliques with and resumes the direct march at the same time as the front rank does, closing to facing distance on arriving in line.

To Face a Line to the Rear and March it to the Rear.

1. *Threes right* (or *left*) *about.* 2. MARCH. 3. *Legion.* 4. HALT. 5. *Left* (or *right.*) 6. DRESS. 7. FRONT. Or, 3. *Guide right* (or *left*).

The Commander passes between the nearest three as they wheel about on a fixed pivot, and places himself two yards in front of the center of the Legion, and the guides wheel into their places.

From a halt to march a few paces to the rear, thus:

1. *Legion.* 2. ABOUT. 3. FACE. 4. *Forward.* 5. *Guide. right* (or *left*). 6. MARCH. Or, if in march, 1. *To the rear.* 2. MARCH. *Guide right* (or *left*).

The guides and Standard Guard step into the rear rank, which has now become the front. Having faced about, number one of each three now becomes number three, and the reverse.

To Break Threes to the Rear.

Marching in line, to pass an obstacle.

1. (So many) *threes from right* (or *left*) *to rear.* 2. MARCH.

At the command *march*, the designated three executes *left forward, threes left* on the three next on its left, which re-

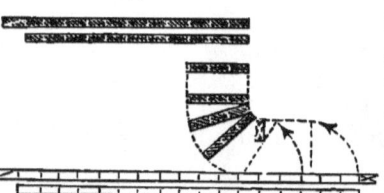

mains in line. The Commander points with his sword to the inner three which leads the movement. The guide, if the threes are broken from his side, closes in on the threes which remain in line; if from the opposite side, the guide on that flank follows in rear of the three next to him.

1. *Rear threes, right* (or *left*) *front into line.* 2. *Double time.* 3. MARCH.

The threes which were broken form in line, and the guide, if on that side, hastens to the point where the right of the Legion will rest.

SCHOOL OF THE LEGION.   59

The Route Step.

Being in column of threes, marching.

1. *Route step.*   2. MARCH.

At this command the swords are carried at will and the Knights need not preserve silence or keep the step, but each covers the file in front and maintains the regular distance.

Change of direction is effected by the same commands as when in the cadence step.

1. *Legion.*   2. ATTENTION.

At the second command the swords are brought to a *carry* and the cadence step is resumed.

To Form Column of Files from Column of Threes.

Being at a halt.

1. *Right* (or *left*) *by file.*   2. MARCH.

At the first command the rear rank, if there be one, closes to facing distance.

At the second command the right file of the leading three of the front and rear rank moves forward, followed in succession by the files on his left. When the left file of the leading three is about to commence the oblique, the right file, front and rear rank, of the second three moves to the front, and so on to the rear of the column, keeping close to facing distance.

The guides (Vice and Lieut.-Commander) precede and follow the leading and rear files.

If marching, the right file of the leading three continues the march, the others halt and resume the march at the proper time. The Commander places himself on the left of the leading guide.

To Form Column of Threes from Column of Files.

Being in march.

1. *Form threes.*   2. *Left* (or *right*) *oblique.*   3. MARCH.

At the command *march*, the leading file of each three, front and rear rank, if there be two ranks, moves forward two yards and halts, the rear rank Knights falling back to twenty-one inches; the other files oblique to the left and place themselves successively on the left of the leading files, the rear rank taking the distance of twenty-one inches from the front rank; the other threes successively form as explained for the first, the leading file of each three halting at twenty-one inches from the correspondig file of the next three in front. The leading guide places himself in front of the left file of the leading three.

To Form Column of Twos from Line, and Line from Column of Twos,

Is executed similar to like formations by threes.

To Form Column of Files from Line, and the Reverse.

In march the command is, 1. *By the right* (or *left*) *flank*. 2. MARCH. If the line is so formed, add: 3. *Guide right*, (*left* or *center*).

From a halt, command: 1. *Right* (or *left*). 2. FACE. 3. *Forward.* 4. MARCH. If by facing the line is formed, add: 5. *Guide left*, (*right* or *center*).

To Form Single Rank from Double Rank.

Being in line.

1. *Form single rank.* 2. *Threes right* (or *left*). 3. MARCH.

All the threes wheel to the right at the command *march*. The front rank of the right threes, upon completion of the

wheel, continues the march, and is conducted by the right guide who is in front of the file on the marching flank; the other ranks halt and successively resume the march when at fifty-four inches, wheeling distance, from the rank preceding.

The rearmost rank having its distance, the Commander commands:

1. *Threes left* (or *right*). 2. MARCH. 3. *Legion.* 4. HALT. 5. *Left* (or *right*). 6. DRESS. 7. FRONT.

Or, 3. *Guide right* (or *left*).

Marching in Column, to Form Single Rank.

1. *Form single rank.* 2. MARCH.

At the second command, the front rank of the leading three continues the march, the others halt and resume the march when at wheeling distance; the rearmost three having its distance, line is formed as before.

If marching in *double time*, or in *quick time*, and the command be *double time*, the front rank of the leading three marches in double time; the others halt and take the double time when at wheeling distance.

The leading guide in column of threes at single rank distance places himself twenty-four inches in front of the file on the marching flank of the leading three. The rear guide follows at the same distance in rear of the file on the marching flank of the rear three.

In single rank the position of the officers are the same as when in double rank. The Legion performs all the movements explained for double rank by similar commands and means.

For small Legions, the single rank formation is recommended.

To Form Double Rank.

Being in single rank.

1. *Form double rank.* 2. *Threes right* (or *left*). 3. MARCH.

At the command *march*, the ranks of threes wheel to the right, the leading rank halts the instant the wheel is completed, the others continue the march and halt successively upon closing the twenty-one inches from the rank preceding.

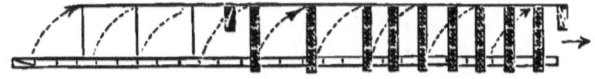

The rearmost rank having gained its distance, the Commander orders:

1. *Threes left* (or *right*). 2. MARCH. 3. *Legion*. 4. HALT. 5. *Left*. 6. DRESS. 7. FRONT. Or, 3. *Guide right* (or *left*).

The command is *threes right* (or *left*), according as the front ranks are on the right or left of their rear ranks. Should the original left three be in front, and its rear rank wanting, the front rank of the succeeding three, instead of closing, remains at its wheeling distance of fifty-four inches.

If the rearmost three is wanting in numbers, to complete it the Lieut.-Commander marches with it when the nature of his duties as guide, etc., does not render it impracticable; but when the Legion is in line, he is in the front rank on the extreme left.

Marching in column of threes, single rank distance, the front rank of each three being in front of its rear rank, *to form double rank*, command:

1. *Form double rank*. 2. MARCH.

At the second command the leading rank halts, the others continue the march, each halting at twenty-one inches from the rank preceding; the rearmost rank having closed, the line is formed as before.

To Close to Double Rank Distance.

Being in march, threes at single rank distance.

1. *Double rank distance*. 2. *Double time*. 3. MARCH.

The leading rank continues in quick time; the other ranks close to twenty-one inches in double time and resume the quick time. If marching in double time the leading rank takes the quick time, as do the others successively upon closing to twenty-one inches.

To Form Column of Divisions.

Being in line at halt.

1. *Divisions right* (or *left*) *wheel*. 2. MARCH.

At the first command the Vice-Commander, as chief of the first division, and the Lieut.-Commander, as chief of the

SCHOOL OF THE LEGION.

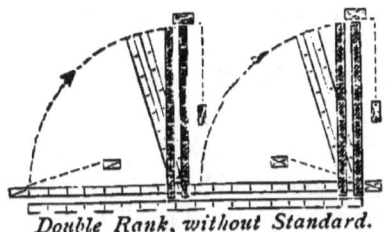
Double Rank, without Standard.

second division, place themselves two yards in front of the center of, and facing, their divisions, and repeat the command, *division right wheel.* At the second command, briskly repeated, each chief of divisions hastens by the shortest line to the point where the left of his division will rest and faces the late rear; the divisions wheel to the right on fixed pivots, and the wheel of each division is conducted as explained in the wheelings of the Legion, the Knights on the right and left of the divisions acting as right and left guides.

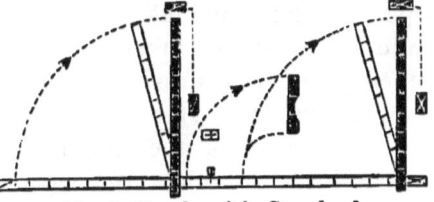
Single Rank with Standard.

When the division approaches the perpendicular, its chief commands:

1. ——*Division.* 2. HALT. 3. *Left.* 4. DRESS. 5. FRONT.

At the command *halt*, the Knights on the left of the divisions place themselves so that their breasts will touch the right arms of their chiefs, who then step back two yards and each dresses his division and places himself in front of its center.

At the command *march*, the Standard Guard also wheels, under direction of the Sen. Work., who is its chief, to the center of the column midway between the divisions.

If in march, the Legion wheels into column by the same commands as at a halt. At the command *march* the pivots halt and mark time in their places, so as to conform to movement of the marching flank.

The position of the Commander is on the side of the guide, four yards from the flank and abreast of the leading division.

Whenever in column a subdivision is dressed, its chief places himself two yards in front of its centre, except the chiefs of threes and sections, who habitually remain on the flanks of their subdivisions.

1. *In three* (or *four*) *divisions.* 2. *Right wheel.* 3. MARCH.

The commander having previously indicated the right and left of the divisions, so that the Standard shall be in the center of the second division, the Vice-Commander commands the leading divisions and the Lieut.-Commander the rear division. At the second command the Senior Workman steps to the front and takes command of the middle division, the Junior Workmen takes the Senior Workman's place, and the left guide of this division quickly fills the interval at the left of the Standard. If in two ranks, the Junior Workman hastens to the right of the Standard Bearer and the number *three* covering the Junior Workman, steps into the front rank on the left of the Standard as soon as the interval is made.

The wheels are conducted as already explained ; at the command *front* the chiefs of divisions place themselves in front of the center of their divisions.

To Form Column of Divisions and Move Forward without Halt.

Being a line at a halt.

1. *Continue the march.* 2. *Divisions right* (or *left*) *wheel.* 3. MARCH. 4. *Forward.* 5. MARCH. 6. *Guide. right* (or *left*).

The divisions wheel as before, except that the chiefs of divisions remain in front of their centers   Each guide preserves his proper distance, and exactly covers the leading guide, who is careful to march straight and keep the correct step and cadence.

To Put a Column of Divisions in Motion and Halt It.

1. *Forward.* 2. *Guide right* (or *left*). 3. MARCH, will put the column in motion from a halt ; and 1. *Legion.* 2. HALT, will halt it.

To Oblique.

The oblique is by the same commands and means as heretofore explained for obliqueing in column of threes.

To Change Direction of a Column of Divisions.

Being in march.

1. *Column right* (or *left*). 2. MARCH.

At the first command the chief of the leading division commands *right wheel;* at the command *march*, repeated by the chief, the division wheels to the right on a movable pivot, the chief adding 1. *Forward*. 2. MARCH, on the completion of the wheel; then adds *guide left* (or *right*), according to the position of the guide before the wheel.

The second division marches squarely up to the wheeling point and changes direction by the same means and commands from its chief.

The Standard Guard wheels on the same ground, under direction of its chief (who does not leave his place on the right), and preserves its place in column.

When the right of a column is in front, the guide is *left*, and the reverse when the left is in front. This is not given as a rule, but as a suggestion, the matter being entirely at the discretion of the Commander.

In changing direction, it is essential that the rear of the column should never be checked; each chief, therefore, whose place is in front of it, faces his division while wheeling, and sees that the guides take the full step of twenty-eight or thirty-three inches, and the pivot nine or eleven inches, according to the time.

The guide in wheeling is always on the marching flank without command; on its completion, each chief of division, or double section, cautions his subdivision *guide left* (or *right*), according as the guide was before the wheel.

Column Half Right (or Left).

Is similarly executed; each chief gives the preparatory command of *right* (or *left*) *half wheel*.

To put a Column of Divisions in March, and change Direction at the same time.

1. *Forward.*   2. *Guide right* (or *left*).   3. *Column right* (or *left*). Or, 3. *Column half right* (or *left*).   4. MARCH.

To Face Column of Divisions to the Rear, and March it to the Rear.

1. *Threes right* (or *left*) *about.*   2. MARCH   3. *Legion.*   4. HALT. Or, 3. *Guide right* (or *left*).

At the fourth command, given the instant the threes complete the wheel, each chief goes to the left of his division and dresses it to the left, commands *front*, and places himself in front of its center.

To march to the rear without halting, the Commander announces the guide when the wheel is nearly completed.

If the column be faced to the rear and one division be smaller than the other, the guide of the second division regains the trace and wheeling distance on the march.

The Standard Guard conforms to these movements and carefully preserves its central position.

The leading division is always the *first division*, whether the right or left is in front.

To Form Line to the Left (or Right) from Column of Divisions.

Being at a halt.

1. *Left* (or *right*) *into line wheel.*   2. MARCH.   3. *Legion.*   4. HALT.   5. *Right* (or *left*).   6. DRESS.   7. FRONT.

The first command is repeated by the Vice and Lieut. Commanders, who promptly take their places on the left flanks of their divisions as guides, the one in the rear exactly covering the one in front.

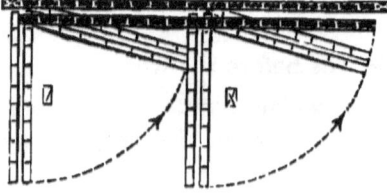

At the command *march* the Vice. and Lieut Commanders turn their heads

SCHOOL OF THE LEGION.

toward their division, repeat the second command, and stand fast; the divisions wheel on fixed pivots.

The Standard Guard wheels conducted by and under direction of chief, so that when the wheel is nearly completed he shall be opposite his place in line.

The Commander commands *halt*, and places himself in prolongation of the line marked by the Vice and Lieut.-Commanders where the marching flank of the leading divisions will rest, and faces the Vice and Lieut.-Commanders.

At the sixth command, the divisions and Standard Guard dress up to the line; at the seventh command, the Vice and Lieut.-Commanders take their places on the flanks of the Legion.

If marching, the movement is executed as just explained, except at the command *march*, the pivots halt and mark time in their places so as to conform to the movements of the marching flank.

To Form Line and Continue March.

1. *Continue the march.* 2. *Left* (or *right*) *into line wheel.*
3. MARCH. 4. *Forward.* 5. MARCH.
6. *Guide left* (or *right*).

The chiefs repeat the commands to, and including, the third, and quickly return to their posts in line, so as to step off with the Legion at the fifth command.

The pivots are careful to *turn* in their places as before, until the wheel is completed.

In long lines the guide may be *center*, when all will dress on the Standard Bearer.

To Form Line on the Right (or Left) from Column of Divisions.

Being in march.

The Commander indicates that the *guide* is *right* or *left*, on the flank toward which the movement is to be executed, and commands:

1. *On right* (or *left*) *into line.* 2. MARCH. 3. FRONT.

At the first command, the chief of the first division commands *right turn;* at the command *march*, repeated by its chief, the first division turns to the right, advances in the new direction, division distance, when the chief halts it, commands,

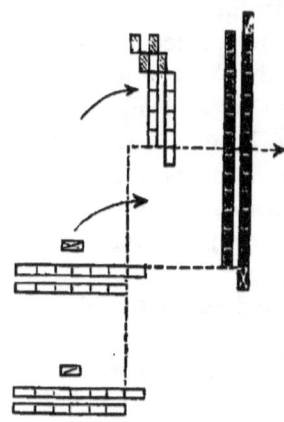

1. *Right.* 2. DRESS, and take his place on its right. The Standard Guard and second division march straight forward, their chiefs successively command *right turn* in time to add MARCH when each is opposite its place in line; they are halted by the chiefs, the Standard Guard when at one and the division when at three yards from the line, who successively command *Right.* DRESS; and when the chief of the second division has given the second command, he takes his post on the left.

The Commander superintends the alignment from the right, and commands *front.*

A similar movement by threes from column of divisions or sections may be executed, as before explained (*vide* page 55); each three in succession breaking from its division by wheeling when opposite its place in line; the command, when in columns of sections or divisions, being preceded by, 1. *By threes.* 2. *On right into line*, etc.

To Break into Divisions.

From a halt.

1. *Right* (or *left*) *by divisions.* 2. MARCH. 3. *Guide left* (or *right*).

At the first command, the Vice and Lieut. Commmanders quickly take their places in front of their divisions; the chief of first division commands *forward;* the chiefs of the Standard Guard and second division command *right oblique.*

SCHOOL OF THE LEGION.

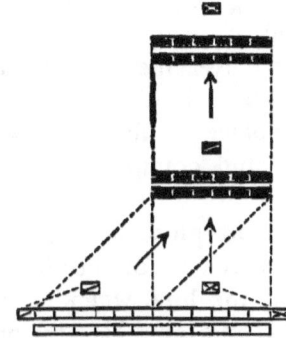

At the command MARCH, repeated by the chief of the right division, the division moves forward, the chief repeating *guide left*. The chiefs of the Standard Guard and left division successively command MARCH when they are severally disengaged, in time to gain their places in column.

The Sen. Work. commands *forward*, and adds MARCH the instant the Guard is opposite the center of the first division, and so regulates the steps that it may immediately gain and preserve its proper distance.

The chief of the left division commands, 1. *Forward*, and adds 2. MARCH. 3. *Guide left*, the instant the Knight on its left arrives in trace of the guide of the leading division; the guide is careful to regulate his steps so as to preserve the proper distance.

If marching, the chief of the first division repeats the command, indicating the place of the guide.

The chiefs of Standard Guard and second division command, 1. *Standard Guard*,(or, 1, *Second division*). 2. *Mark time;* repeat the command MARCH, adding *right oblique* in time to command MARCH when they are disengaged; the movement is completed as from a halt.

To Re-form the Legion.

Being at a halt.

    1. *Form Legion.* 2. *Left* (or *right*) *oblique.*
    3. MARCH. 4. FRONT.

At the second command the chief of the first division commands, 1. *Forward*. 2. *Guide right*. The chiefs of the Standard Guard and second division command, *left oblique*.

At the command MARCH, repeated by the chiefs, the first division advances division distance, when its chief commands,

1. *First division.* 2. HALT. 3. *Right.* 4. DRESS, and returns to his place on the right flank.

The Guard obliques to the left, its chief commanding 1. *Forward* in time to add 2. MARCH. 3. *Guide right*, the instant the guard is opposite its place in line. When in rear of the line its chief halts it and commands, 1. *Right* 2. DRESS.

The second division marches to its place in line by the same commands and means as prescribed for the Standard Guard, halting at three yards from the line, when its chief commands, 1. *Right.* 2. DRESS, and takes his post on its left.

The Commander superintends the alignment from the right, and gives the fourth command.

If marching in *quick time*, and the command be *double time*, the Commander commands, *guide right* (or *left*) immediately after the command *march;* the chief of the leading division commands, 1. *Forward*, 2. MARCH, and repeats the indication for the guide. The chiefs of the Standard Guard and second division repeat the commands *double time*, MARCH, and when they are about to arrive in line, command *quick time*, adding MARCH the instant they are abreast of the leading division. The divisions and guard united, the Vice and Lieut. Commanders return to their posts on the flanks.

If marching in *double time*, the chief of the first division, at the first command of the Commander, commands *quick time*, repeats the command MARCH, and also the command for the guide.

To March a Column of Divisions by the Flank and Re-form the Column.

Being at a halt.

1. *Right* (or *left*). 2. FACE. 3. *Forward.* 4. MARCH.
5. *Guide*   right (or *left*).

The Vice and Lieut. Commanders place themselves in front of the leading files, and the guard marches in columns of files in the center between the divisions. The Commander is on the side of the guide, four yards from the flank, abreast of the chiefs of divisions, or on a line midway between them.

If in march, the divisions may be moved to the right or left by the commands, 1. *By the right* (or *left*) *flank*. 2. MARCH. 3. *Guide right* (or *left*).

Or, *if at a halt, or in march*, by the command:

1. *Threes right* (or *left*). 2. MARCH. 3. *Guide left* (or *right*).

The Vice and Lieut. Commanders quickly place themselves in front of their divisions, as in columns of threes; the Standard Guard wheels as other threes do, and maintains its central position.

To Form in Column Again.

If the divisions are marching by the flank in columns of files, command, 1. *By the left* (or *right*) *flank*. 2. MARCH. 3. *Guide left* (or *right*).

If marching in columns of threes, as explained, the Commander commands:

1. *Threes left* (or *right*). 2. MARCH. 3. *Guide left* (or *right*). Or, 3. *Legion*. 4. HALT.

The threes and Standard Guard wheel to the left into column of divisions; the Vice and Lieut. Commanders take their positions and exact distances are carefully preserved.

If halted, the chiefs dress their commands and promptly take their places in front of the centers of their divisions.

To Advance by the Right or Left of Divisions from Line.

1. *Divisions*. 2. *Right* (or *left*) *forward*. 3. *Threes right* (or *left*). 4. MARCH. 5. *Guide right* (or *left*).

At the second command the Vice and Lieut. Commanders

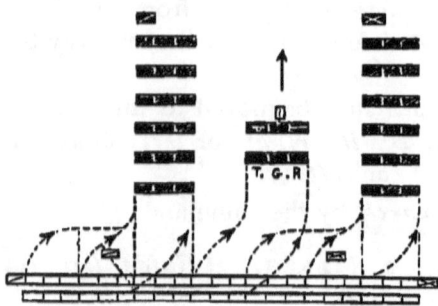

quickly place themselves in front of the centers of their divisions. At the command MARCH, each division executes the movement from its right. The chiefs place themselves in front of the left files of the leading threes, the Commander is midway between on a line with the Vice and Lieut. Commanders.

The Standard Guard wheels to the right, and follows the division whose rear file is next to it, until it is opposite the center between the divisions, when it wheels to the left and marches into its place in the center, under direction of its chief.

To Form in Line again.

1. *Divisions.* 2. *Left* (or *right*) *front into line.* 3. MARCH. 4. *Legion.* 5. HALT. 6. *Right* (or *left*) 7. DRESS. 8. FRONT.

The Vice and Lieut. Commanders hasten to their posts on the flanks.

The Standard Guard obliques to the left, halts in rear of its place in line, under the direction of its chief, and dresses to the right. The command *halt* is given when the leading threes have advanced division distance.

To Form Column of Threes from Column of Divisions.

1. *Divisions.* 2. *Right* (or *left*) *forward.* 3. *Threes right* (or *left*). 4. MARCH.

The Vice and Lieut. Commanders take their places in columns of threes. The Standard Guard marches straight forward and wheels to the right, so as to follow the leading division as it passes.

To Form Column of Divisions from Column of Threes.

1. *Divisions.*   2. *Left* (or *right*) *front into line.*   3. MARCH.
4. *Legion.*   5. HALT.

At the second command the Vice and Lieut. Commanders place themselves on the left and opposite the centers of their divisions.

At the third command each division executes *left front into line;* the chiefs place themselves in front of the centers of their divisions ; the Standard Guard obliques to the left and marches to the center between the divisions, under direction of its chief. The command *halt* is given when the leading division has advanced division distance ; each chief dresses his division to the right, and takes his place in front of its center.

If executed in double time, or in quick time, and the command be *double time*, the Commander commands, *Guide right* (or *left*), immediately after the command MARCH.

Legion and Display Drill.

REMARKS. Thus far the movements have been chiefly legitimate or assimilated to the U. S. Infantry Tactics, substituting *threes* for *fours*, *divisions* for *platoons*, dispensing with *file closers*, causing the Vice and Lieut. Commanders to perform the double duty of lieutenants and sergeants, and providing for a Standard Guard.

The movements which follow are in harmony with the principles laid down.

As it is not desirable to describe minutely every detail that may arise in the movement of a Legion, the Commander will use his discretion in supplying any detail or omission. His decision should be final in any case not supplied by the tactics.

The Standard Bearer may carry the standard, dispensing with others of the guard, but his movememts will be similar to those of the full guard. If the Standard Bearer does not carry the standard, the Guard should fall in as other Knights.

In small legions the commands of the chiefs of small subdivisions, in the display drill, may be dispensed with, if so directed.

How to Determine Position in Column.

When *ones count*, as at the formation of the Legion, it is to number the threes. The odd threes being the right and even threes the left of sections. Hence the number of the section and position of any three therein is instantly ascertained by dividing the number by two. An odd three at the rear of the column marches in rear of the left three of the rear section; or the Vice-Commander counts *one* and the Lieut.-Commander marches with the rear section on its left flank, with number two of the left three wanting, if they are so directed.

It is unnecessary to *count twos*, although it may be done if desired, as *one* and *two* from the right of each section form the first two; number *three* of the right three and *one* of the left three of each section form another two; and numbers *two* and *three* of the left three of each section form the next two.

To Form Column of Threes by a Flank Movement from Column of Files.

Being in march,

1. *Left* (or *right*) *flank by threes*. 2. MARCH.

At the first command the Vice-Commander places himself twelve inches to the left of number three of the leading three, faced in the direction toward which the column is marching. At the command MARCH both the Vice-Commander and the leading three march by the left flank; the others move forward until each three in succession has gained the ground from which the first three marched by the flank, when it executes the same movement, follows in trace of the three next in its front, and maintains its proper distance in the column. The Lieut.-Commander turns to the left, following the left file of the rear three.

To Form in Line, Faced to the Rear, from Column of Threes.

1. *Right* (or *left*) *front into line, faced to rear.* 2. MARCH. 3. *Legion.* 4. HALT. 5. *Right* (or *left*). 6. DRESS. 7. FRONT.

The movement is executed as previously explained for *right front into line*, except that at the command *halt* the leading three wheels *left about* on a fixed pivot and dresses toward the point of rest; the other threes successively wheel about on the same line and dress as before explained.

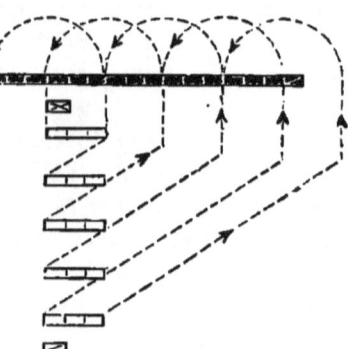

A similar movement may be made from column of sections, except that the sections do not halt until three yards beyond the line; the sections are then wheeled, threes left about, by the chiefs, who successively command *right dress;* the Commander verifies the alignment, and commands FRONT.

This will reverse the order of threes, but the following consecutive movements will place them in their original position in column of sections:

Form column of threes, by the commands *threes right* or *right forward threes right*, etc., then *form sections right oblique,* hereafter explained.

To Form Line by Two Movements from Column of Threes.

A part of the column having changed direction to the right, to form line to the left, the Commander commands:

1. *Threes left.* 2. *Rear threes left into line.* 3. MARCH.

Those threes which have changed direction execute *threes left*, halt and dress to the right, at the command of the chief of the leading division; the rear threes execute *left front into line*, and dress upon the established line at command of the chief of the rear division; at the completion of the movement the Commander commands *front*.

To Form Line, Faced to the Rear, by two Movements.

A part of the column of threes, having changed direction to the right as before, the Commander commands:

1. *Threes right.* 2. *Rear threes left front into line, faced to rear,* 3. MARCH.

The threes which have ·changed direction wheel to the right, halt and dress to the left at the command of the chief of the leading division; the rear threes execute *left front into line, faced to rear*, obliqueing far enough to the left of their places in line that in wheeling about they shall come squarely up to their proper positions and dress on the new alignment.

At the completion of the movement the Commander commands *front.*

If the column has changed direction to the left, the line is formed to the right by inverse command, thus:

1. *Threes left.* 2. *Rear threes right front into line, etc.*

To Change Front.

Being in line.

1. *Change front on right* (or *left*) *three.* 2. *Threes right* (or *left*). 3. MARCH. 4. *Legion.* 5. HALT. 6. *Right.* 7. DRESS. 8. FRONT.

At the the third command the threes wheel to the right; the Vice-Commander quickly places himself on the right of the first three and, with it, moves straight to the front; the others oblique to the left and successively march to the front when opposite to their places in line. The command *halt* is given when the leading three has advanced Legion distance, and the movement is completed as in *left front into line.*

1. *Change front forward on right* (or *left*) *three.* 2. *Threes right* (or *left*). 3. MARCH. 4. *Legion.* 5. HALT. 6. *Right.* 7. DRESS. 8. FRONT.

At the command MARCH, the threes wheel to the right; the first three advances a distance equal to its front and halts at

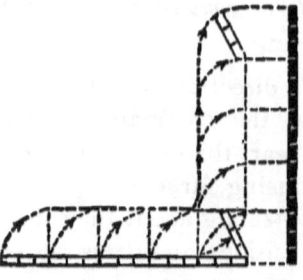

the fifth command; the other threes advance until they execute the same movement as in *right forward, threes right*, wheeling to the left from the ground traversed by the right three in its wheel to the right, and the movement then is completed as in *on right into line*.

To Form Line on the Standard Guard from Column of Threes.

1. *On Standard into line.* 2. *Threes right about.* 3. *Rear threes, left front into line.* 4. MARCH.

At the fourth command the threes in front of the standard wheel to the right about, and execute *left front into line,*

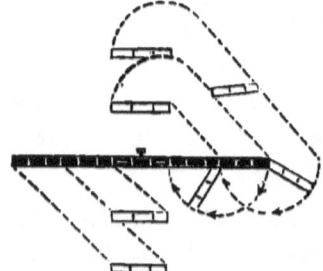

faced to rear, obliqueing to the left of their places in line a distance equal to their front, so that in wheeling about, after passing the new line, they shall be opposite their places and not lap over on the Standard Guard.

The rear threes execute *left front into line* as before explained.

If in march, the Sen. Work. at the fourth command, orders his guard to halt. Dress on the center.

To Wheel about the Standard from Column of Files.

Being in march.

1. *On Standard left wheel.* 2. *By the left and right flanks.* 3. MARCH.

At the command MARCH, given as the left foot strikes the ground, the Standard Bearer advances, plants the right foot and *halts;* the Knights in his front execute *by the left flank*, and immediately commence the *left wheel* about him. The Knights in rear of the Standard face to the right, into line, and commence the left wheel about the Standard. Each wing being careful to preserve the alignment with the other. When the wheels are nearly completed the Commander orders: 1. *Left wing to the rear.* 2. MARCH. 3. *Legion.* 4. HALT. 5. *Center.* 6. DRESS. 7. FRONT. At the command *halt*, given as the right foot strikes the ground, the right wing halts; the left wing executes *to the rear march*, bringing the left foot to the side of the right, and *halts;* the Standard Bearer faces about, and the line is dressed on the center or either flank.

To Wheel in Line from Column of Threes.

1. *Threes left* (or *right*). 2. *Left* (or *right*) *wheel.* 3. MARCH. 4. *Legion.* 5. HALT. 6. *Right* (or *Left*), 7. DRESS. 8. FRONT.

The threes wheel to the left; and the instant they are united in line the Legion wheels to the left on a movable pivot, as before explained, and is halted, or marched forward by the usual commands and means.

To form Column of Sections.

From a halt, being in line.

Sections right (or *left*) *wheel.* 2. MARCH. 3. *Legion.* 4. HALT. 5. *Left* (or *Right*). 6. DRESS. 7. FRONT.

At the second command each section wheels on a fixed pivot; the Vice-Commander moves to a place about forty-four inches in front of the point at which the left file of the leading section will rest, and faces to the left (rear of column); the Lieut.-Commander marches straight forward, halts and faces to the right, on the prolongation of the line upon which the left files of each section will rest, when the wheel is completed; the Vice and Lieut.-Commanders are now facing each other; the Standard Guard wheels to the center of the column, between the sections which were on its right and left, before the movement commenced.

At the command *halt*, given as the sections approach the quarter circle, the left files step promptly up to the place where the left of their section will rest and on a line between the Vice and Lieut.-Commanders, facing the Vice-Commander, each opposite the chief of his section, perpendicular to its former position; the Vice and Lieut.-Commanders see that the guides cover each other; the chiefs of sections, without moving out of their places, superintend the alignment of their sections, the commands being given by the Commander.

At the seventh command the Vice-Commander in front faces about and the officer in rear closes up to forty-four inches from the left file of the rearmost section.

If marching: At the second command the Vice and Lieut.-Commanders hasten to their places in column; the pivots halt, mark time in their places, and conform to the movements of the marching flank. Chiefs of sections, from their places on the right, without turning the head, see that in all movements their sections keep dressed and preserve the proper step and distance, the cautions being given in a low tone of voice, and only when necessary.

To Wheel into Column of Sections from Line and Advance without Halting.

1. *Continue the march.* 2. *Sections right* (or *left*) *wheel.* 3. MARCH. 4. *Forward.* 5. MARCH. 6. *Guide right* (or *left*).

The sections wheel as before, except that the Vice and Lieut.-Commanders take their posts in the column, and the Commander gives the fourth command in time to add MARCH the instant the sections arrive at the perpendicular from the former front.

To form Column of Sections from Column of Threes.
Being in march.

1. *Form sections.* 2. *Left* (or *right*) *oblique.* 3. MARCH. 4. *Guide left* (or *right*).

At the third command the odd threes take a short step and *mark time;* the even threes oblique to the left, until opposite their places in sections, when they resume the *forward march.* The Commander gives the fourth command the instant the threes are united in sections, and all take the full step.

If the threes are reversed, that is, when the odd become the even threes in the column of threes, sections are formed upon the same principles, but to the right. The command being, 1. *Form sections.* 2. *Right oblique,* etc. Or, 1. *By section.* 2. *Threes right.* 3. MARCH. Explained below.

To Form Column of Sections to the Left or Right, from Column of Threes.

Being in column of threes, marching, the Commander commands:

1. *By section.* 2. *Threes left (or right).* 3. MARCH.

At the second command the Vice-Commander quickly places himself on the left of the second three.

At the command MARCH the Vice-Commander advances 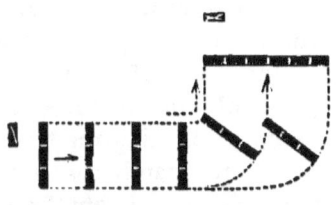 and wheels in front of the file on his right; the leading and second three wheel to the left on movable pivots, uniting in section on the completion of the wheel and marching perpendicular to their former direction. The other threes advance and, by section, execute the same movement on the same ground; the Standard Guard advances and wheels to the left in rear of the center of the section in its front. The Lieut.-Commander shortens his steps as the rear threes wheel and follows in the column of sections as explained before.

To Break into Column of Threes from Column of Sections.

1. *Right by Threes.* 2. MARCH. 3. *Guide left (or right.*

At the command MARCH, the right threes move straight forward; the left threes, as soon as disengaged, oblique to the right into column of threes, the Vice and Lieut.-Commanders and Standard Guard also obliqueing to their places; and the threes that oblique resume the forward without command, as soon as the left file of the three has gained the trace of the leading guides.

To halt after the formation of the column, the Commander immediately commands after *march*, *Legion*, and adds *halt* the instant the left files of the obliqueing threes have gained the rear or the left files of the threes in their front. The columns halt, and those that obliqued face to the front.

To Form Column of Threes to the Right or Left, from Column of Sections.

Being in march.

1. *By section.* 2. *Threes right* (or *left*). 3. March.

At the second command the Vice-Commander quickly places himself twenty-one inches in front of the left file of the right three; at the command *march* he wheels to the right, as if he was the marching flank of a rank of three leading the column; the threes of the leading section execute *threes right*, following the trace of the Vice-Commander; the rear sections march forward, and each in succession executes the same movement from the same ground. The Standard Guard wheels on the same ground to its place in the column; the Lieut.-Commander closes to his place, twenty-one inches from the left file of the three in rear.

To March in Line.

Before the movement of threes from column of section is completed, commaud:

1. *Threes left.* 2. *Rear section forward*, and add 3. March, the instant the rearmost section is about to wheel by threes; the threes that have changed direction execute *threes left;* the rear section marches straight forward, and as the line is

formed, the Commander commands, *guide right* (or *left*). The Standard Guard wheels as a rank of three.

Or the line may be formed thus:

1. *Threes left.* 2. *Rear sections left front into line.* 3. *Double time.* 4. MARCH. 5. *Guide right.* Or, 6. *Legion.* 7. HALT. 8. *Right.* 9. DRESS. 10. FRONT.

And the movement is executed upon the principles before explained; the seventh command being given when the right threes have advanced Legion distance.

To Form Columns of Threes from Column of Sections, and March to the Rear.

1. *Threes right and left about.* 2. MARCH. 3. *Guide Center.*

At the second command the right threes execute the *right about*, and the left threes the *left about*, on fixed pivots; the Standard Guard executes the movement, *to the rear, march*, and regulates its steps so as to maintain its place; the Vice-Commander turns to the right and places himself directly in the rear (after the about) of the Standard Bearer, advancing quickly until he is abreast of and between the rearmost threes. The Lieut.-Commander also turns himself to the right and places himself on a line with the Vice-Commander and Standard Bearer, and abreast of and between the leading threes. The Commander marches two yards in front of the Lieut.-Commander. The threes of each section carefully preserve section distance and the alignment with each other.

1. *Form section.* 2. *Threes left and right about.* 3. MARCH. 4. *Guide left.*

At the command MARCH the threes wheel about on fixed pivots re-uniting the sections, the guard executing *to the rear, march*, as before. The Vice and Lieut.-Commanders resume their places and the guide is then announced. Or,

1. *By threes.* 2. *Front to rear.* 3. MARCH. 4. *Guide center.*

LEGION AND DISPLAY DRILL.

Being in column of sections, marching.

At the third command the threes of the leading section wheel from the center *right and left about* and march to the late rear, the pivots describing circles whose radii are 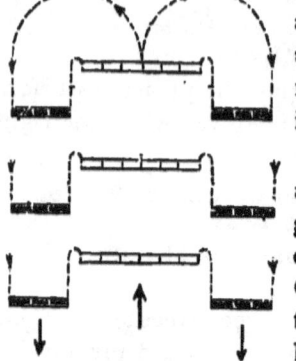 twelve inches; the others advance and the threes of each section in succession execute the same movement on the same ground, thus forming two columns of threes.

The Standard Guard will advance and wheel about, on the same ground, into the column that wheeled to the right; the Vice and Lieut.-Commanders place themselves twenty-one inches in front of the left files of the leading threes, the Vice-Commander in advance of the column that wheeled to the right about, and the Lieut.-Commander taking his place in lead of the other column as it passes. The Commander marches between and on a line with the Vice and Lieut-Commanders at the head of the column.

1. *Form sections.* 2. *Front to rear.* 3. MARCH.

This is given after the columns of threes are formed, as just explained, as soon as the heads of the column have passed the rearmost section, or may be deferred. At the third command the leading threes wheel about toward the center, unite in section and march toward their former rear; the others in succession execute the same movement on the same ground, following in column of sections; the officers resume their places, and the Standard Guard, after wheeling, obliques to its place in center.

To Close Sections to Half Distance or in Mass.

Being in column.

1. *To halt* (or such) *distance close column.* 2. MARCH.

At the command MARCH the leading section stands fast, if at a halt, or halts if in march, at the caution of its chief; the others advance and successively halt at the given distance and are promptly dressed at command of the chiefs of sections.

If in line, command:

1. *To half* (or such) *distance close column.* 2. *Sections right* (or *left*) *wheel.* 3. MARCH.

At the third command the sections wheel to the right and the leading section is halted and dressed by its chief; the others advance, on completing the wheel, and the movement is completed as before explained.

These movements may be executed in double time; then the leading section continues the march in quick time, after the wheel is completed; the others close successively to half distance and take the step and cadence, from the guide in their front, at the command *quick time, march*, by the chief of their section.

To Take Wheeling Distance from Column of Sections in Mass, etc.

1. *Take wheeling distance.* 2. MARCH.

At the second command the leading section marches forward, at the caution of its chief; the others halt, if in march, or stand fast if at a halt, and successively take up the march, at the commands of their chiefs, when the designated distance is gained.

To Form Column of Sections, Forward, from Line.

1. *Center forward.* 2. *Threes left and right.* 3. MARCH. 4. *Guide right* (*or left.*)

At the second command the Vice-Commander places himself in front of the left file of the center section. At the command MARCH the center section and Vice-Commander move straight forward; the threes of the right wing execute *left forward threes left*, and those of the left wing execute *right forward threes right;* the Leiut.-Commander follows the column of threes on the left, falling back to his place in column of sections, as the rear threes unite in section.

If the Standard Guard is present, the Vice-Commander places himself in front of its left file and the Guard and Vice-Commander lead the movement.

Column of sections may be formed thus when the original right is the center of the line.

To Form Line to the Front, from Column of Sections.

1. *Right and left front into line.* 2. MARCH. 3. *Legion.* 4. HALT. 5. *Center.* 6. DRESS. 7. FRONT.

At the command MARCH the Standard Guard (or center section) marches straight to the front; the right threes execute *right front into line* and the left threes execute *left front into line.*

The line may be formed in this way from column of sections when the original center of the Legion is at the head of the column, and may be executed in double time on principles before explained.

To Form Line by Two Movements, from Column of Sections at Half Distance.

1. *Threes right* (or *left*). 2. *Left* (or *right*) *threes on right* (or *left*) *into line.* 3. MARCH. 4. FRONT.

At the command MARCH the right threes execute *threes right*, move forward Legion distance and the Vice-Commander commands, 1. *Right wing* (or *First division*). 2. HALT. 3. *Right.* 4. DRESS, and takes his place on the right. The left threes execute *on right into line*; the Lieut.-Commander quickly placing himself in front of the leading three, commands, 1. *Left wing* (or *Second Division*). 2. HALT. 3. *Right.* 4. DRESS, giving the second command as the leading three of the left wing arrives in rear of its place in line, and places himself on the left, in prolongation of the line. On completion of the movement the Commander commands *front*.

The movement may be executed without halting, thus:

1. *Threes right.* 2. *Left threes on right into line.* 3. *Double time.* 4. MARCH. 5. *Guide right.*

The left threes execute the movement as before explained, but in double time, taking the step and alignment from the right wing as they successively arrive on the line. The Commander commands *guide right* when the right threes have united in line, they then advance in quick time.

To Form Line by Three Movements from Column of Sections.

1. *By section.* 2. *Threes right and left.* 3. MARCH.

Being in column of sections at half distance. At the command MARCH the left three of the leading section wheels to the left and the right three wheels to the right, marching in opposite directions; the other sections advance and, except the one in the rear, successively execute the same movements from the same ground. The Vice-Commander is in lead of the right threes, and the Lieut.-Commander quickly places himself in lead of the left threes as before explained, when the movement is commenced. [If the Standard Guard is in the column, it does not wheel, but marches straight to the front and *marks time* on a line with the marching flanks of the threes that wheeled into columns right and left.] When the rearmost section approaches the point from which other sections broke into threes, the Commander commands:

1. *Into line.* 2. *Threes left and right.* 3. MARCH.
4. *Guide center.*

At the second command the chief of the section that has not broken cautions it to *forward*, and at the command MARCH, given the instant the rear section has gained the ground from which the others wheeled by threes, this section marches straight forward; the threes on its left wheel to the right, those on the right wheel to the left into line, the

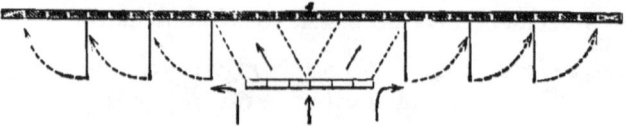

Commander announces the guide and places himself two yards in front of the center of the Legion.

[If the Standard Guard is present, the command MARCH is given, so that the rearmost section may break and its threes oblique to your right and left of the Standard Guard.]

Column of Sections may then be Formed by the Commands:

1. *Center forward.* 2. *Threes left and right.* 3. MARCH, as before explained.

The column is now left in front with the original left threes still on its left, the Vice-Commander in advance. To cause the threes to occupy their original position in column of sections, right in front, repeat the commands for the formation of line by three movements, and the formation of column of sections on the center forward as before; or consecutive movements indicated by the following commands: 1. *Threes right* (or *left*) *about.* 2. MARCH. Each three wheels on a fixed pivot and, reuniting in section, the column marches to the late rear, then: 1. *By section.* 2. *Threes left.* 3. MARCH.

To Form Column of Twos, from Column of Sections.

1. *Center forward.* 2. *Files left and right.* 3. MARCH.

At the command MARCH the left threes execute *right forward files right*, and the right threes execute *left forward files left;* the Standard Bearer marches forward and the others of the Guard form a rank of two in his rear, all maintaining the same distance. It now being a column of files, double rank, the leading files shorten the steps until the Commander, seeing the rear files have closed to their

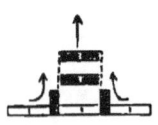
places, commands *forward, march,* when all take the twenty-eight inch step.

To form into column of sections again, command:

1. *Right and left front into sections.*
2. MARCH.

The right files of each section execute *right front into line,* and the left files of each section execute *left front into line,* thus re-forming each section; the rear sections shorten the steps until each in succession has gained its proper distance.

Similar movements from the center of double sections may be made by similar commands and means.

To Wheel in Circles for Display.

From column of sections.

1. *Threes in circle right and left wheel.* 2. MARCH.
3. *Guide left* (or *right*).

At the command MARCH the Vice-Commander takes two steps to the front and halts; the Lieut.-Commander steps backward the same distance and halts; the right threes wheel on fixed pivots to the right, numbers one marking time, and conforming to the movement of the marching flank; the left threes wheel to the left in like manner on numbers three. When the circles are completed and the sections re-formed, the column moves forward at the command for the guide. The Standard Guard marks time in its place until the sections are re-formed, then marches forward.

Great care should be taken in executing the wheels, so that each three will complete the quarter circle at the same instant; also in re-forming the sections and commencing the *forward, march,* at the same instant.

To Wheel One-half of the Sections at a Time.

Being in march.

1. *Right threes in circle, right wheel.* 2. MARCH.

At the command MARCH the right threes wheel as just described, and when completed march forward as before; the Standard Guard, by *right side steps*, places itself in rear of the wheeling threes and marks time until the circle is completed then follows the three in its front, When the wheel is nearly completed the chief commands, 1. *Left threes in circle, left wheel,* and adds, 2. MARCH, so that the left threes will commence the wheel the instant the right threes resume the *forward, march.* When the left threes complete the wheel, the sections will be re-united, if the movement is executed properly; the column moves forward without command and the Standard Guard obliques to the left into its place.

Similar movements may be executed when marching in line, and by similar commands and means.

To Advance Even Sections to the Front of Odd Sections in Column.

1. *Threes in circle, right and left wheel.* 2. *Even sections forward.* 3. MARCH.

At the command MARCH the right threes of the first, third, and other odd sections wheel in circles to the right, and the left threes of the same sections wheel in circles to the left on movable pivots, each pivot Knight describing a circle whose radius is twelve inches; the second, fourth, and other even sections march straight forward, passing between the threes of the section in their front as they complete the half circle. The Vice-Commander shortens his steps and moves forward; the Lieut.-Commander follows the rear section, if it be an even section, and halts when he has gained the distance of two yards from the section that is wheeling by threes; when the movement is completed he closes to fifty-four inches from the left file of the rear section and follows the column; if the rear be an odd section, he takes two backward steps and halts as before. When the wheeling threes have completed their circles and re-unite in sections, they march forward and are careful to regain the proper distance if lost.

To move the former odd, now the even, sections forward into their original places in column, the commands and movements are exactly similar to those just explained.

[If the Standard Guard is in the column, it advances between the wheeling threes; the sections regulating the steps so as to maintain their positions. The Commander commands, 1. *To the rear.* 2. MARCH, repeats the movement just explained, and again executes *to the rear, march,* which brings the Standard to its original position.]

The Deploy Column of Sections.

Being at a halt.

1. *On first section deploy column.* 2. *Left.* 3. FACE. 4. *Forward.* 5. MARCH. 6. FRONT.

At the first command the Vice-Commander faces about and places himself on the right of the first section, whose chief commands, *stand fast*, and immediately dresses it to the right. The other sections face to the left at the third command.

At the command MARCH the Standard Guard and all the sections, except the first, being faced to the left, march straight forward; the chief of the second section commands, 1. *By the right flank*, and adds, 2. MARCH. 3. *Guide right* the instant he is opposite his place in line. This section halts in rear of the line at command of its chief, who immediately adds, 1. *Right.* 2. DRESS.

The guides of the rear sections march abreast of each other and parallel to the second; each chief in succession marching his section *by the right flank*, and dressing it upon the line as described for the second section. The Lieut.-Commander hastens to the point where the left of the line will rest; the Commander superintends the alignment and commands *front*.

If marching command, 1. *On first section deploy column.* 2. *By the left flank.* 3. MARCH. At the third command the first section is halted and dressed by its chief; the rear sections and guard march by the left flank, and the movement is completed as before.

    1. *On fourth* (or rear section, naming it) *deploy column.*
    2. *Right.* 3. FACE. 4. *Forward.* 5. MARCH.
                   6. FRONT.

Being at a halt

At the first command the Vice-Commander faces and marches to the right, halts and faces about in front of the chief of the first section; the Lieut.-Commander hastens to place himself in the post vacated by the Vice-Commander and faces him; the chief of the fourth section commands, *Fourth section stand fast.*

At the command FACE the other sections face to the right. At the fifth command the rear section marches straight forward, halts one yard from the Vice-Commander and its chief dresses it upon the Vice and Lieut. Commanders; the Vice-Commander faces about, marches in prolongation of the line, halts where the right of the Legion will rest, and again faces about exactly in front of the Lieut.-Commander, facing him. In the mean time the other sections move forward, at the fifth command, led by their chiefs, at section distance, parallel with each other; the guide of the third section commands, 1. *Third section.* 2. *By the left flank*, and adds, 3. MARCH. 4. *Guide left*, the instant the fourth section is unmasked. When within one yard from the established line its chief halts it and immediately commands, 1. *Third section.* 2. *Left.* 3. DRESS, when it dresses upon the line.

When the guide of the third section commands *by the left flank, march,* the second section advances section distance and then marches by the left flank in the same manner, and is dressed as described for the third section, and so on with the remaining section.

The Commander commands *front* when the movement is completed, and the Vice and Lieut.-Commanders take their places in line.

If marching the commands would be, 1. *On fourth section deploy column.* 2. *By the right flank.* 3. MARCH. 4. FRONT.

The fourth section continues to march straight forward at the caution of its chief; the others march *by the right flank*, and the movement is completed as before.

It is of great importance in all deployments that commands be promptly given and distances accurately maintained.

1. *On* (such a) *section* (or Standard Guard) *deploy column.* 2. *Right and left.* 3. FACE. 4. *Forward.* 5. MARCH. 6. FRONT.

Being at a halt.

At the command MARCH the sections in front of the designated section, deploy to the right; those in rear deploy to the left. The designated section, as soon as unmasked, is marched forward at command of its chief to the line established by the Vice and Lieut.-Commanders, as bebefore described (p. p. 92), and is dressed to the right against the Vice and Lieut.-Commanders, who then face about and march in prolongation of the line, halt where the right and left of the line will rest, and each faces toward the other. The other sections are dressed toward the designated section, and the movement is completed upon principles before explained.

If in march, the designated section is halted in rear of the line; the sections in front of the designated section are marched *by the right flank;* those in rear are marched *by the left flank,* and the movement is completed as before.

To Form Double Sections from Column of Sections.

Remarks:—The first and second sections form the first double section; the third and fourth sections form the second double section, and so on.

The Vice-Commander is chief of the leading double section, the Lieut.-Commander chief of the one in rear. If there are three double sections, the Senior Workman takes command of the second. If there are four double sections, the Standard occupies the center of the second and the Senior Workman commands it, the Junior Workman commands the third. If more than four, the Senior Workman commands the center double section having the Standard; the Junior Workman commands the one in its rear. The Knight on the right acts as chief of double section unprovided for. When double sections are dissolved the chiefs resume their places. The Standard Guard may retain its identity and march between the double sections that were on its right and left if desired; or it may form the left three of a section, in which event it will execute the movement with its section. Or, the Standard Bearer alone may march as if the full guard was with him. These various positions are determined by the number of Knights in line.

Being at a halt the Commander orders:

1. *Form double sections.* 2. *Left oblique.* 3. MARCH.

At the second command the chiefs of the odd numbered sections command, 1. *Forward.* 2 *Guide right,* and the chief of the even numbered sections command *left oblique.* At the command *march,* repeated by the chiefs, the odd sections advance section distance; their chiefs command, 1. *Section.* 2. HALT. 3. *Right.* 4. DRESS. The even sections oblique to the left, their chiefs commanding, 1. *Forward,* in time to add, 2. MARCH. 3. *Guide right,* the instant each is opposite his place in line. When one yard from the line, the chiefs command, 1. *Section.* 2. HALT. 3. *Right.* 4. DRESS. The chief of each double section superintends the alignment of his double section, commands *front*, and places himself two yards in front of its center.

The Standard Guard (or Standard Bearer alone if the "guard" be not with him) obliques to the center of the column between two double sections; or the Standard Bearer hastens to place himself between the two sections in his front (or rear) as they unite; the others of the guard taking post on the flanks, or taking command as has just been explained, and as previously may have been directed by the Commander.

If in march, double sections are formed by the same commands and means, except that the even sections are not halted and dressed; the odd sections, instead of halting at the section distance, *mark time* at the command of their chiefs, and the chief of each double section commands, 1. *Forward,* adding 2. MARCH. 3. *Guide left.* the instant the sections have joined.

To Break into Sections from Column of Double Sections.

1. *Right by sections.* 2. MARCH. 3. *Guide left.*

At the first command each chief of double section repeats *Right by section,* and resumes his place in column of sections; the chief of each right section turning his head toward it, but without moving out of his place, commands, *Right section forward;* the chiefs of each left section in like manner command, 1. *Left section.* 2. *Mark time,* repeats the command MARCH, immediately commands *right oblique,* and adds MARCH, so that each even section may commence the oblique as soon as it is disengaged, adding *forward, guide left* when it has gained its place in column.

To Wheel Subdivisions and the Legion in Circles Consecutively without Halting.

1. *Threes in circle right* (or *left*) *wheel.* 2. MARCH. 3. *Sections in circle left* (or *right*) *wheel.* 4. MARCH. 5. *Double-sections in circle right* (or *left*) *wheel.* 6. MARCH. 7. *Divisios in circle left* (or *right*) *wheel.* 8. MARCH. 9. *In circle right* (or *left*) *wheel.* 10. MARCH. 11. *Legion.* 12. HALT. 13. *Left.* 14. DRESS. 15. FRONT; Or, 11. *Forward.* 12. *Guide right* (or *left*). 13. MARCH.

At the second command each three wheels in a full circle to the right on a fixed pivot. When the circle is nearly completed the third command is given in time to add MARCH the instant the threes are re-united in line, and each section, in like manner, wheels on a fixed pivot in full circle. The Standard Guard so conducts its wheel on a movable pivot that it will exactly unite with the sections as the line is formed each time. When the sections are united in line the second time, that is, having completed the circle, the sixth command is given;(the preparatory commands in each case being given so as to add the command of execution as directed). At this each double section wheels to the right in a complete circle, and on a fixed pivot, the Standard Guard wheeling as before but in larger circles. When the double sections unite in line as the circle is completed, the eighth command is given, and the divisions wheel as described for double-sections, the Standard Guard wheeling as before described. The line being again re-formed, the Legion is wheeled on a movable pivot by the ninth and tenth commands. In all the wheelings the command MARCH is given the instant the line is re-formed, after the circle is completed, so that the smaller subdivisions re-form the line after the full about, instantly break with the next larger subdivisions, continue the wheelings in the opposite direction and so on.

The Vice and Lieut.-Commanders do not wheel with the subdivisions, but face and march from the center in prolongation of the line, or close toward it and face to the proper front on the flanks, so that when the half circle is completed, in each wheel, except the last, they, with the subdivision, will, for the instant only, be in perfect line faced to the late rear; the Vice and Lieut.-Commanders marking time, the subdivisions continuing the wheel; when they are disengaged the Vice and Lieut.-Commanders face and retrace their steps, again completing the line faced to the original front the instant the full circle is finished, and so on until the wheel is by Legion front, when they remain on its flanks.

This may be executed in part, if desired, omitting such of the wheels as may be deemed expedient or desirable.

To Change Direction of Column, of Sections (Double Sections or Divisions).

1. *Change direction by the right* (or *left*) *flank.* 2. *Threes right* (or *left*). 3. MARCH.

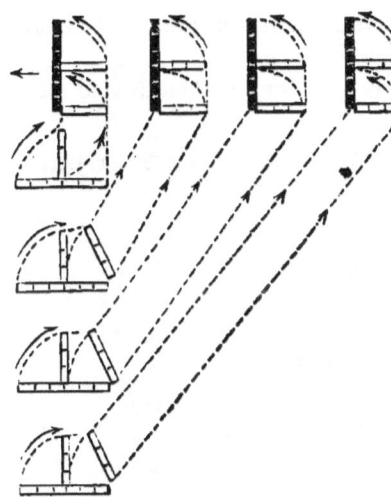

At the second command the chief of the first section commands, 1. *First section.* 2. *Right forward.* 3 *Threes right.*

At the command *march* the first section executes *right forward, threes right;* when the rear three completes the wheel to the left, the Chief commands, 1. *Threes left.* 2. MARCH. 3. *Section.* 4. HALT. 5. *Left.* 6. DRESS. 7. FRONT

The other sections wheel by threes to the right or half right, and are so conducted by the chiefs as to enter the new column parallel to the first section. As each section arrives in rear of the one next preceding, it is formed in line to the left and dressed to the left. The Vice and Lieut.-Commanders quickly gain their places in the column and assist in the alignment of the guides, as heretofore explained.

If the column be of double sections or divisions, each chief halts when near the point where the left of his division will rest in column, and allows his division to march past him.

To Advance by the Right or Left of Double Sections.

Being in line.

1. *Double sections.* 2. *Right* (or *left*) *forward.* 3. *Threes right* (or *left*). 4. MARCH. 5. *Guide right* (or *left*).

At the third command the Vice-Commander places himself in front of the left file of the first three; the Lieut.-Commander quickly places himself in front of the left file of the right three of the double section on the left of the Legion. The other chiefs of double sections take the same relative position, and the movement is completed as explained for divisions.

Line or column is formed by similar commands and means as are described for divisions.

To Break by Right of Subdivisions to the Rear into Column.

Being in line at a halt.

1. *Right of sections, rear into column.* 2. *Threes right.* 3. MARCH. 4. *Threes left.* 5. MARCH. 6. *Legion.* 7. HALT. 8. *Left.* 9. DRESS. 10. FRONT. Or, 6. *Guide left.*

At the first command the chief of each section cautions the right three that it will have to *right about.* At the third command the threes will wheel to the right on fixed pivots. The right three of each section will then change direction to the right (late rear) on a movable pivot; the other three of

LEGION AND DISPLAY DRILL. 99

each section moving forward and changing direction on the same ground as its right three. The Commander, seeing the movement nearly completed, commands, 4 *Threes left*, in time to add 5. MARCH, the instant the left of the left threes has reached the line lately occupied by the Legion, and adds, 6. *Legion*. 7. HALT. The left guides of sections exactly cover each other under direction of the Vice and Lieut.-Commanders and the chiefs of sections; at the tenth command the Vice and Lieut.-Commanders take their proper places in column. If the command for the guide is given, the column moves forward without halting.

The Standard Guard wheels about and marches into its place in column, then wheels to the left, regulating its steps so as to maintain its place.

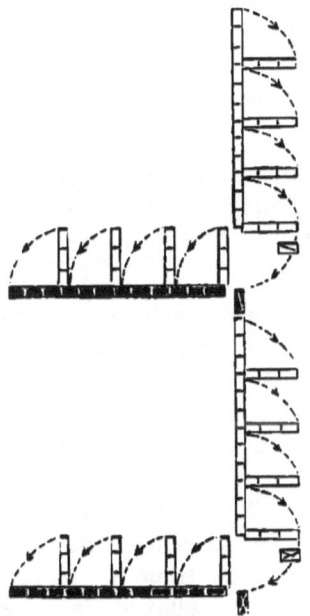

Divisions (or double sections) break to the rear into column from line by similar commands and means, except that the chiefs of divisions, etc., at the first command place themselves in front of their divisions, and caution the first three as before, repeat the third command, place themselves on the marching flank of the leading three in their divisions, wheel with it and halt on the late line, so that the file on the marching flanks of the next threes, in passing to the rear, will graze the chief's right arm. When the rear three nearly completes the wheel, each chief of divisions (or double section) commands, 4. *Threes left*. 5. MARCH. 6. *Divisions* (or *double section*). 7. HALT; the left guide of the division places himself so that his arm will lightly touch the chief's left breast, who then gives the eighth, ninth and tenth commands (in lieu of Commander, as explained for the same movement by sections), and places himself in front of the center of his division or double section.

Similar movements by files, without the wheelings of threes, being at a halt, are made thus:

The Commander commands, 1. *Right of sections rear into column.* 2. *Right.* 3. FACE. 4. *Forward.* 5. MARCH. 6. *Legion.* 7. HALT. 8. *Left.* 9. FACE. 10. *Left.* 11. DRESS. 12. FRONT. Or, 6. *By the left flank.* 7. MARCH. 8. *Guide left.*

At the third command the Knights at the right of sections (chiefs) come to an *about face*, and at the fifth command move straight to the rear; the others follow, turning on the same ground. When the last Knight or file is about to turn to the rear, the Commander halts the Legion, faces it to the left, and dresses it as explained, or marches it by the left flank into column.

1. *Right of sections rear into column.* 2. *By the right flank.* 3. MARCH. 4. *By the left flank.* 5. MARCH. 6. *Guide left.*

Being in line marching.

At the third command the right file of each section executes *to the rear, march*, and marches straight to the rear; the others face and march to the right. On arriving at the point where the right file marched to the rear, each file of that section in succession follows in his trace, being careful to keep closed to facing distance, each section executing the same movement at the same instant. The fifth command is given the instant the last files are about to turn to the rear, so that they do not in fact turn but continue to march straight forward; or the command may be delayed until he turns to the rear, so that all march by the left flank at that command.

The officers take their positions as heretofore explained.

Divisions and double sections are formed into column by files from the right of divisions to the rear, by similar commands and means.

To Deploy Column of Double Sections.

Being at a halt.

1. *On first double section deploy column.* 2. *Threes left* (or *right*). 3. MARCH.

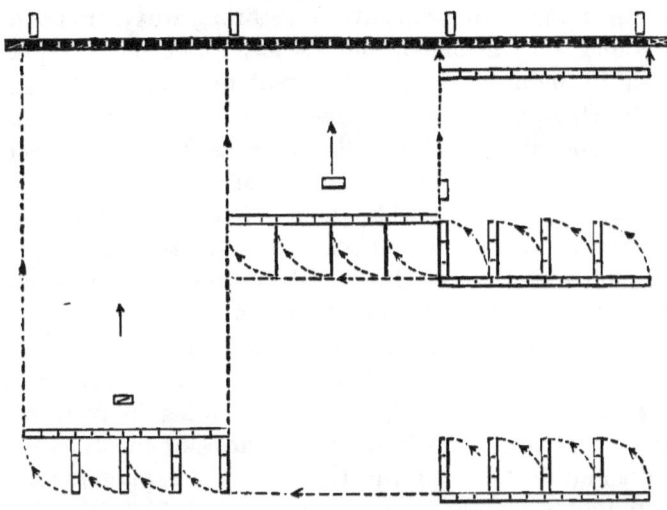

At the first command the chief of the first double section cautions it to *stand fast*, and places himself three yards in front of his place on the right; the left guide steps three yards straight to the front; the other chiefs repeat *threes left*, and quickly place themselves two yards in front of the left guides, facing the left. At the command MARCH the chief of the first double section commands, 1. *First double section.* 2. *Right.* 3. DRESS. 4. FRONT; at the third command it dresses on the line between the chief and left guide. The double sections wheel by threes to the left, the chiefs repeating the command MARCH. The chief of the second double section stands fast, and when the left of his double section approaches him, commands, 1. *Second double section.* 2. *Threes right.* 3. MARCH. 4. *Guide right.* The third command is given the instant the front rank of the rear three (if there be two ranks, or if not, then when the rear three) arrives opposite the place of the right file when in line. On approaching the line the chief commands:

1. *Second double section.* 2. HALT.

At the command HALT, given at three yards from the line, the double section halts, and its left guide quickly places himself on the line where its left will rest, and at the same time the chief, if his place in line is on its right, places himself 22 inches from, and on a line with the Knight on the left of the first double section, aud commands. 1. *Right.* 2. DRESS. 3. FRONT. The guide of the third double section marches abreast of and parallel to the second; its chief having advanced two yards, after the command, *threes right, march,* from the chief of the second, halts, in his own person, and when the right of his double section approaches him, commands, 1. *Third double section.* 2. *Threes right.* 3. MARCH. 4. *Guide right,* and, marching in front of its center, conducts it to within three yards of the line, when he halts and dresses it to the right, as just explained for the second double section.

If there are more than three double sections, the others execute the movement as described for the second and third.

If marching, the chief of the first double section halts it at the command MARCH, and the movement is executed as before.

1. *On third double section deploy column.* 2. *Threes right* (or *left*). 3. MARCH.

Being at a halt.

At the second command the chief of the third double section cautions it to stand fast.

At the command MARCH all the double sections, except the third, wheel by threes to the right, the chiefs repeating the second and third commands; the chief of the first double section conducts his double section to the right in prolongation of its former front; the chief of the section halts oppo-

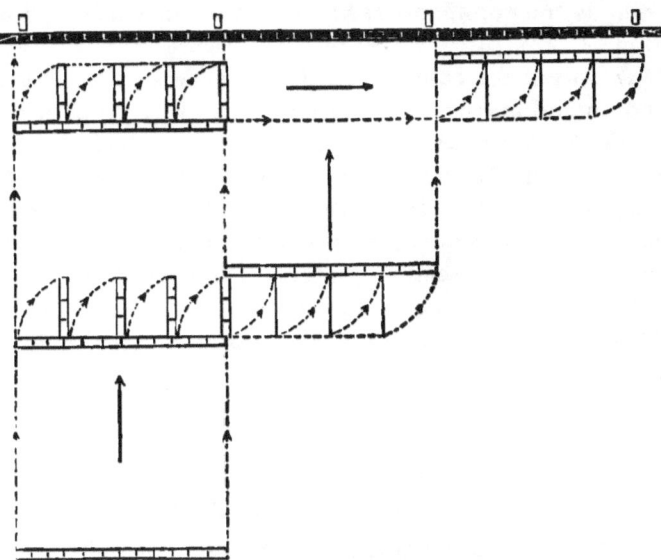

site the right of the third, and when the rear of his double section approaches, commands. 1. *Second double section.* 2. *Threes left.* 3. MARCH. 4. *Double section.* 5. HALT.

The third command is given the instant the third double section is unmasked.

The chief the third double section, when he sees it nearly unmasked, commands, 1. *Third double section.* 2. *Forward.* 3. *Guide left.* 4. MARCH. When this double section reaches the ground from which the first one moved to the right, the chief commands, 1. *Third double section.* 2. HALT. At the command *halt* the chief and left guide quickly place themselves three yards in front of their places in line, and the chief commands:

1. *Third double section.* 2. *Left.* 3. Dress. 4. Front.

If there are more than three double sections, each conforms to what is explained for the second, and each is conducted to the line and dressed as explained for the third.

The chief of the first dresses his double section to the left as soon as the command *front* is given to the second double section

If in march the chief of the third double section halts it at the command *march;* the movement is executed as before.

To deploy the column faced to the rear on the first or third double section, without first causing it to wheel about by threes, the Commander adds, *faced to rear* after *deploy column.* The movement is executed as already explained, except each double section marches three yards beyond the line, then wheels about by threes and halts, after which it is dressed toward the double section upon which the deployment is made.

Deployments on Interior Double Sections.

1. *On* (such) *double section (Division* or *Standard Guard) deploy column.* 2. *Threes right and left.* 3. March.

At the command March the double sections in front of the one designated deploy to the right; those in rear deploy to the left. The designated double section, as soon as unmasked, is conducted on the line of the first double section with the guide right, and is dressed to the right. The other double sections are dressed toward the designated double section.

To Deploy Column of Threes in Open Order.

Being in march.

1. *On right three* (so many yards) *take distance.*
2. March.

At the second command the leading three marches straight forward; the others halt. When the second three has gained six yards (if the number is not given in the command) from the three in front, it resumes the full step at the command *forward, march*, by its chief, and so on in succession to the rear of the column.

The Commander then commands:

1. *On center deploy.* 2. MARCH. 3. *Guide center.*

The Knight in the center of each three and the Standard Bearer march straight to the front, shortening the steps. The Knights on the flanks oblique to the right and left until an interval of three yards from the center is gained, when all turn and march straight forward, taking the full step. The guides are the center Knights, who are careful to preserve their intervals and distances.

The Vice aud Lieut.-Commanders place themselves in front and rear of the center on a line with the guides, and three yards (or one-half the given distance) from the advance and rearmost three.

To Deploy Column of Sections, etc.

Distance from the right is gained as just explained.

1. *On right* (or *left*) *center deploy.* 2. MARCH. 3. *Guide center.*

The movement is executed as in column of threes, except that the Knights on the right of the center, according to the command, march straight forward, the others oblique right and left as commanded. The Standard Bearer marches forward so as to occupy, as near as practicable, the center of the column; the others of the guard oblique to the right and left to the given interval. The Vice and Lieut.-Commanders are in front and rear of the center as before, and on a line between them is the Standard. The guides are the Knights on whom, or from whom, the deployment was made.

To Close into Column Again.

1. *To full distance close column and intervals.* 2. MARCH.

The Knights on the flanks oblique toward the center, and when they have gained their places in threes (or other subdivisions from which deployment was made), again march to the front, being careful to preserve the alignment and exactly cover the corresponding Knights in front, closing to wheeling distance immediately; the leading threes shorten the steps, as do each three in succession, when they have gained the proper distance. At the command *forward, march,* all resume the twenty-eight inch step; the Vice and Lieut.-Commanders also regain their places, so as to be ready to step off with the column at the command.

To Close on the Center only.

Without distributing the distance between the threes the Commander commands:

1. *On center close intervals.* 2. MARCH.

The Knights gradually regain their positions on the center, re-forming threes, by oblique steps gaining ground forward, keeping the shoulders square to the front and maintaining the alignment.

To Close Threes to Wheeling Distance.

Before or after closing the intervals between the Knights of each three the Commander commands :

1. *To wheeling* (or such) *distance close column.* 2. MARCH.

The files in front shorten their steps, and when the threes are close to the designated distance, as before explained, the Commander commands *forward, march,* and all take the twenty-eight inch step.

If the command be *double time,* the leading three continues the march in *quick time,* those in the rear close in *double time,* until having gained the distance indicated, each in succession marches in quick time, taking the step from the guide in front.

To Deploy Line by Files to the Front.

1. *On Standard* (*right* or *left file*) *deploy.*   2. MARCH. Or, 2. *Double time.*   3. MARCH.

At the second command the Standard Bearer advances by short steps straight to the front; the Knights on the right oblique to the right, those on the left oblique to the left until each in succession has gained an interval of three yards from the Standard, or the Knight next to them toward the Standard Bearer, when they turn and march to the front, dressing toward the center, which should never be passed. When all have arrived in the line, the Commander commands, *formard, march*, and all take the full step.

If the command be *double time*, the Standard Bearer advances with the full step; the others oblique as described, but in double time, taking the step from the Standard Bearer as they arrive on the line.

To Deploy Line in Open Order by the Flank.

1. *By the right* (or *left*) *flank take intervals.*   2. MARCH. 3, *Legion.*   4. HALT. Or, 3. *By the left* (or *right*) *flank.*   4. MARCH.   5. *Guide right*, (*left* or *center.*)

Being in line, single rank.

At the second command the Legion faces to the right and, if in march, halts; the Vice-Commander alone continues the march in prolongation of the former line; the others follow successively at the distance of three yards, each steadily in trace of his predecessor, until the Knight, or Lieut.-Commander, in rear of the column has reached his interval, when at the fourth command all halt, pause the ninetieth of a minute, face to the former front. Or,

The line is re-formed and moves to the front, at the command *by the left flank, march.*

1. *On Standard* (*right* or *left center*).   2. *By the right and left flank take intervals.*   3. MARCH.   4. *Legion* 5. HALT. Or, 4. *By the left and right flank.* 5. MARCH.   6. *Guide center* (*right* or *left*).

Being in line, single rank.

The Commander points with his sword to the center file on which the movement is to be made, and at the third command those on its right face to the right; those on its left face to left, and the movement is executed upon the principles before explained.

To Extend Intervals.

1. *By the right* (or *left*) *flank to* (so many) *yards extend intervals.* 2. MARCH. 3. *Legion.* 4. HALT.

Or, 3. *By the left* (or *right*) *flank.* 4. MARCH.

The movement is executed as before explained.

If desired to deploy from line or column to a greater interval than three yards, the number of yards is stated in the command, and the movement is executed on the same principles.

To Close the Intervals by the Flank.

1. *By the left* (or *right*) *flank close intervals.* 2. MARCH.

At the command MARCH, the left guide stands fast (or if in march, halts), the others march by the left flank and successively halt and face to the front upon closing to their places.

To March Files to the Rear from Column of Threes at Open Order (Deployed).

Being in march.

1. *To the rear.* 2. MARCH. Or,
1. *Counter-march.* 2. *By files right* (or *left*). 3. MARCH.

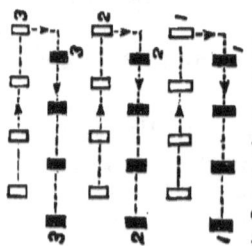

At the second command the Vice-Commander faces to the right, and having arrived opposite the center, between numbers one and two, again faces to the right and marches to the rear. As he turns to the rear the Commander commands MARCH, at which the leading number two faces to the right, and when in rear of the Vice-Commander, turns and follows in his trace; number three of the leading three turns to the right, and when he arrives at a point half way between the place from which he turned and the place just occupied by number two, he faces and marches to the rear. Number one executes the same movements, turning to the rear when he has gained ground to the right equal to one-half the interval between his own position and that of number two before the movement commenced. The others advance and follow exactly in trace of their fraters in front, turning on the same ground.

The alignment and intervals should be carefully preserved, and the wheelings by threes, etc., may be executed by commands, etc., similar to those before explained.

Order in Echelon.

Being in line at a halt (or in march).

1. *Threes* (or *sections*) *on center* (*right* or *left*) *front into echelon.* 2. MARCH. 3. *Guide center* (*right* or *left*).

At the first command the Senior Workman cautions the Standard Guard to 1. *Forward.* 2. *Guide center*, and the chiefs of other threes caution, *stand fast* (or *halt*); at the command MARCH, the Standard Guard marches straight forward; when it has advanced fifty-four inches the threes next on its right and left, at the caution of their chiefs,

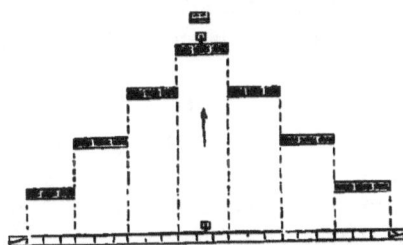

given in a low tone, take up the march, and so on until the entire line is in march.

The Knight on the right and left of each three toward the center is the guide of his three, and should be careful to preserve the designated distance from the Standard or preceding three, and exactly opposite his place in line, as well as to keep dressed on the three opposite to him.

The Vice and Lieut.-Commanders also take up the march at the prescribed distance, and the Commander places himself in front of the Standard at the same distance, or may march in rear of the Standard on a line with the Vice and Lieut.-Commanders.

If the Commander desires the distance to be greater or less, he adds to the first command, after the word "center," *at* (so many) *yards distance*, and the movement is similarly executed.

Sections in echelon are similarly executed.

1. *Threes* (or *files*) *on right* (or *left*) *of division front into echelon.* 2. MARCH. 3. *Guide right* (or *left*.)

Being in line.

Each division executes the movement as explained for the Legion, the right three of each division marching forward at the second command; the second three of each division moving forward as explained when the first has gained fifty-four inches, and so on. The Vice-Commander places himself on the right of the leading three of the first division; the Lieut.-Commander quickly places himself on the left and abreast of the rear three of the left division.

The Standard Guard maintains its place in the center abreast of the leading three.

To March in Echelon to the Rear.

1. *Threes right* (or *left*) *about.* 2. MARCH. 3. *Guide right* (or *left*).

The Vice and Lieut.-Commanders wheel as number three of a rank of three into their places *in echelon*.

To March in Echelon by the Flank.

1. *Threes right* (or *left*). 2. MARCH. 3. *Guide right* (*left* or *center*.)

The Vice and Lient.-Commanders wheel so as to gain the same relative position, when the movement is completed.

Sections may be wheeled to the right or left, changing direction in echelon.

To Re-form the Line.

1. *On center* (or such a subdivision) *front into line.* 2. MARCH. 3. *Center.* 4. DRESS.

At the first command the chief of the leading subdivision cautions it that it will have to halt; the chiefs of other threes or subdivisions, to the right and left in rear of the center, command *forward,* and repeat the command *march,* at the same time the chief of the leading subdivision commands it to halt; the threes on each side of the center halt and dress toward the center on arriving in rear of the line, so that the threes opposite each other *in echelon* will halt and dress at the same instant. When the last three has dressed, the Commander commands, *front.*

To Form Sections in Echelon from Threes in Echelon.

Threes being in march at four yards distance in echelon, command:

1. *Odd threes in circle right wheel.* 2. MARCH.

At the command MARCH, the first, third and other odd threes wheel to the right, on fixed pivots, completing full circles; the even threes continue the march and unite in sections with the odd threes the instant they have completed the circle, and the sections move forward in echelon without halting. The sections may be wheeled by similar commands and means, forming double sections in echelon, which may also be wheeled in like manner, forming divisions, and so on, until the line is formed. Or,

Line is formed by commands and means before explained.

To Form in Echelon from Column of Files.

Being in march, double rank.

1. *Files right and left into echelon.* 2. MARCH.

At the command MARCH, the two leading Knights place

themselves about one foot apart, and then by short steps march straight forward; the other left files oblique to the left, each in succession resumes the *forward march*, without command, when his right shoulder shall exactly cover the left shoulder of the Knight next in front. The right files gain ground to the right in similar manner, the left shoulder of each exactly covering the right shoulder of the Knight next in front The Standard Guard forms in line and marks time at command of its chief until it gains its proper place in the center and on a line with the rearmost Knights (Vice and Lieut.-Commanders) in the columns; the Vice-Commander quickly places himself at the right and rear of the right column, and the Lieut.-Commander at left and rear of the left column of files *in echelon.*

The Commander commands *forward*, adding MARCH the instant the movement is completed, and places himself in front of the leading files.

If the lines are small, ground is gradually gained to the right and left, the Knights keeping the shoulders square to the front, as they may have been previously instructed by the Commander; or, he may indicate it by giving as the first command, *files bear right and left into echelon.*

To Re-form Column of Files.

1. *Files right and left into column.*   2. MARCH.

At the first command the Vice-Commander takes his place at the head of the column.

The leading Knight advances by shortened steps; the others oblique toward the center, regulating the step so that each double file will successively re-unite, then, turning to the front, will follow in trace of those immediately in their lead. The Standard Guard marches forward to its place.

To Open and Close Ranks in Echelon from Line.

1. *By turns.*   2. *Threes front into echelon.*   3. MARCH.

At the third command, given as the right foot strikes the ground, the left threes of each section *mark time*, the right threes advance until the right foot has been planted the third time (*i. e.* six steps), when they too mark time; the rear threes having planted the right foot the third time, step off with the left foot, pass between the threes in their front, and advance six steps in front of them, being twelve steps from their first position, when they mark time again, and so on by turns until the Commander desires the line to advance together, when he commands, 1, *Forward.* 2. *Guide right* (or *left.*) 3. MARCH; the third command being given the instant the line is re-formed.

The Vice and Lieut.-Commanders successively advance with the threes in front.

Or, he commands, *odd threes in circle right wheel,* adding MARCH the instant the line is formed, when the odd threes wheel full about; the even threes march between the wheeling threes, which advance as soon as they complete the circle.

If the Commander desires the threes to march in column, he commands *threes right* (or *left*) is time to add MARCH the instant the threes are united in line. Or the line may be halted the instant it is re-united, and is dressed by the usual commands.

To form Line Obliquely and Files in Echelon from Threes in Echelon, or Sections in Column.

Being *on right in echelon*, marching (represented by the left half of plate, page 109), command:

1. *Threes half left into line.* 2. MARCH. 3. *Guide right.*

At the command MARCH the threes wheel to the left one-eighth of a circle. The leading three having wheeled, marches straight forward, shortening the step a little; the Vice-Commander places himself on its right; the others oblique to the right, preserving the line with the right three until each in succession has closed the interval, when it marches to the front and dresses to the right. As the last three, with the Lieut.-Commander on its left, faces to the front, the Commander commands, 1. *Forwad*. 2. MARCH, and all take the full step.

If the line is a short one, the leading three takes the full step, the rear threes, if so instructed, may lengthen their steps until the intervals are closed, the command to forward march being omitted.

If the threes are in echelon, center in front, as represented in the plate (page 109), the command is:

1. *Threes half right and left into line.* 2. *Rear threes by the left and right flank close intervals.* 3. MARCH. 4. *Left and right oblique.* 5. MARCH.

The Standard Guard being in front, as a set of three.

At the third command the leading three halts; its flank files face half right and left, outwardly, and take one twenty-two inch side step to their right and left, from number two; the right threes wheel to the right forty-five degrees, then face and march to the left, successively closing the intervals toward the center of the Legion (now the apex of triangle with two sides), halt and face to the right into line; the left threes half wheel to the left, face and close the intervals to the right and *left face* into line, both lines dressing upon the Knights at the apex of the triangle; the Vice and Lieut.-Commanders close on the rear, or flanks farthest from the center of the Legion.

At the fourth command both lines *half face* toward the center; that is, to the same front as when the movement was commenced, and at the fifth command all march forward, preserving the distance and triangular form of the echelon movement.

Column of sections may be formed into echelon of files by similar commands and means (omitting the second command);

LEGION AND DISPLAY DRILL. 115

the leading section breaks by threes half right and left and halts; the others wheel in like manner and advance obliquely into line and halt; they are then marched to their former front by the last two commands. The Vice-Commander may form the angle in front, or goes to the rear, as before, according to previous instructions.

General Remarks, Apropos.

In the formation of figures, etc., no rigid rules can be given, as the number of officers or Knights, the presence of the Standard Bearer alone, or of the full guard, would necessitate some modification in each case by the officer in charge, or interminable explanations in the tactics.

The commands of the chiefs of threes are in fact merely cautions to enable the threes to move together, and may be dispensed with if so instructed by the Commander. *This rule is general*, and may be applied to sections at the discretion of the officer in charge.

To Form Column Again.

1. *Form column*. 2. MARCH.

At the command MARCH, numbers one and three of the Standard Guard take their places at the side of the Standard Bearer, and the guard marches forward by short steps; the leading files of the right threes face to the left and march to the center, followed by their comrades of the same three; the leading files of the left threes face and march to the right, followed by the others of their threes. The threes of each section unite at the center, face toward the head of the column, and regulate the steps so as to gain their proper distance. When all the sections have united, the Commander commands, 1. *Forward*. 2. MARCH. 3. *Guide left* (or *right*.

Column of threes may be formed by similar commands and means when the right or left is in front, *in echelon*.

To Form Line from Files in Echelon.

Line to the front is formed by means and commands similar

to those explained on page 110; the files obliqueing opposite their places, then march straight to the front, halting in rear of the line and dressing toward the point of rest.

To Form Cross from Column of Threes.

Being in march, single rank.

1. *Form Cross.*   2. MARCH.   3. *Forward.*   4. MARCH.
5. *Guide center.*

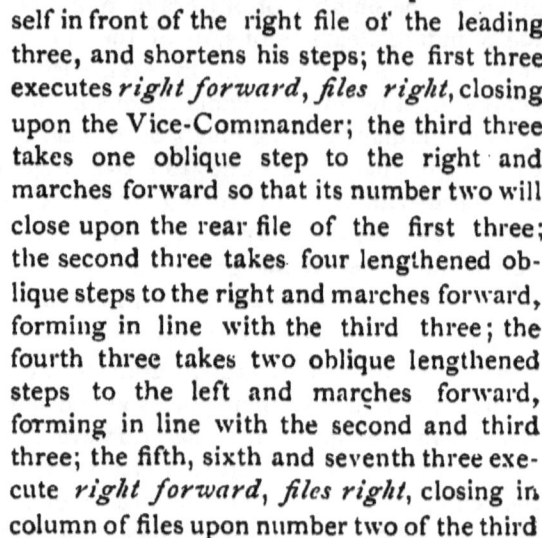

At the second command the Vice-Commander places himself in front of the right file of the leading three, and shortens his steps; the first three executes *right forward, files right*, closing upon the Vice-Commander; the third three takes one oblique step to the right and marches forward so that its number two will close upon the rear file of the first three; the second three takes four lengthened oblique steps to the right and marches forward, forming in line with the third three; the fourth three takes two oblique lengthened steps to the left and marches forward, forming in line with the second and third three; the fifth, sixth and seventh three execute *right forward, files right*, closing in column of files upon number two of the third three. The threes shorten their steps upon arriving in their places. The Lieut.-Commander follows in rear of the column. Seeing the movement completed, the Commander gives the concluding commands, and places himself at the head of the cross.

If there be but five threes, the movement is similarly executed, the third three forming the left arm of the cross.

If there are eight threes, with the Standard Guard in the column, the first and second threes form the upper arm of the cross; the third three obliques to the right, the fourth three obliques to the left; the Standard Guard obliques twenty-two inches to the right and marches straight forward; the four threes in rear form the lower arm of the cross, upon principals explained before. At the command MARCH the Vice-Commander quickly places himself on the right of the third three, and the Lieut.-Commander quickly places himself on the left of the fourth three, so that the Vice and Lieut.-Commanders will be on the flanks of the horizontal arm of the cross and the Standard at the angles in its center. The Select Commander marches about four yards to the left and abreast of the Lieut.-Commander, or at the top as before. Cross from column of sections is formed by similar commands and means.

Supernumerary threes close in column as the base of the cross, or may form in triangle, etc., as hereafter explained, the command being, 2. *Rear threes form triangle*, etc.

To Reduce Cross to Column

Of like subdivisions from which it was formed.

1. *Form column.* 2. MARCH. 3. *Guide left.*

At the command MARCH the threes that are in column of files execute the *left front into line;* the first three continues the march, the second three *left obliques* into column; the third three *marks time*, until it is disengaged, when it obliques into its place in column; the fourth three *right obliques* to its place. The threes having re-formed, the column *mark time*, when their guides are in trace of the guide in front, and successively advance as each gains its distance.

The Select Commander gives the third command as soon as the movement is completed.

To Form Greek Cross from Column of Sections, etc.

The arms of a Greek Cross are so nearly equal that the difference is not readily perceived. The same number of threes, sections, etc., form each arm of the cross; usually the Standard Guard is in the center, the Vice-Commander at the top (in advance), and the Lieut.-Commander in rear at the base. These may be changed when necessary to equalize the limbs of the cross.

1. *Form Greek Cross.* 2. MARCH. 3. *Guide center.*

At the first command the sections execute the following movements, the chiefs giving the commands if necessary to insure prompt action: First and fourth sections *right forward, files right,* forming the advance and rear arms of the cross; second section and Standard Guard *right oblique,* forming the right arm and center; third section *left oblique,* forming the left arm, as described before for the Passion Cross.

Creek Cross, from column of threes and double sections, is formed by similar means, the chiefs giving the commands for their double sections, causing them to take the short step, to march forward, etc., at the proper time. As the cross is completed the chiefs promptly take their places, and the cross moves forward at the command of the Commander.

To Reduce Greek Cross to Column

From which it was formed, command: (See also p. 136).

1. *Form column.* 2. MARCH. 3. *Guide left.*

At the first command the following movements are executed as indicated by the commands, viz:

First and fourth sections. *Left front into line.*
Second section and Standard Guard. *Left oblique.*
Third section. *Right oblique.*

And the movement is completed as explained for the Passion Cross.

To Form Greek and Passion Cross from Column of Threes.

The Vice and Lieut.-Commanders, Standard Guard and eight threes being in the column, marching.

1. *Form Cross.* 2. *Leading threes form Greek Cross.* 3. MARCH. 4. *Guide center.*

At the command MARCH the four threes nearest to the head of the column form Greek Cross, the first and fourth threes executing *right forward, files right;* the second three obliques to the right and the third three obliques to the left, forming the several arms of the cross, as before explained, the Vice-Commander quickly placing himself in its center; the Senior Workman places himself forty-four inches to the front and shortens his steps; the Standard Bearer quickly takes the place thus vacated, and the Junior Workman places himself between the two; the Lieut.-Commander quickly places himself in front of the Senior Workman, and the cross is formed as before explained, with the Standard in its center.

The Select Commander places himself at the head of the Passion Cross and commands, *forward,* MARCH, and all move forward.

Care should be taken to preserve the proper distance between the two crosses, which will result from the same step being taken by the Select Knights at the heads of both.

The cross is reduced by commands and means similar to those before explained.

Supernumerary threes may form at the base, as shown in illustration (2), or may form a second Greek Cross. In the latter case the second command would be, 2. *Leading and rear threes form*, etc.

The crosses are reduced by the commands, etc., as before.

To Display Greek Cross and Reduce it to Column again.

Being in column, marching.

1. *Display Greek Cross*. 2. MARCH. 3. *Guide center*.

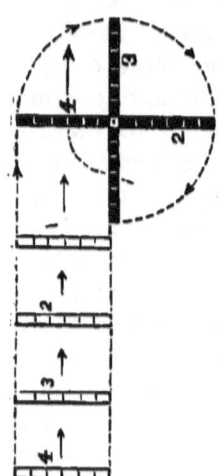

At the command MARCH the Vice-Commander continues the march full two yards straight forward and halts; the leading section wheels to the right (or left, according to previous instructions) in a complete circle, the pivot Select Knight taking short steps, so as to describe a circle of about one yard in diameter; the three sections in its rear march forward until each in succession has gained the ground from which the first section commenced the wheel, when each wheels, following exactly in trace of the preceding section. The chief of the leading section commands *forward*, in a low tone, in time to add MARCH the instant it has gained the ground from which it commenced the wheel, and this section marches straight to the front; the others follow it in column from the same point. These commands should be loud enough to be heard only by the section to whom they are addressed, that the cross may appear to dissolve without command.

The guide is then on the same flank that it was before the movement commenced, and without command.

The Lieut.-Commander places himself on the left of the fifth section, and during the display the rear sections *halt* at his command, given the instant before the fourth section commences, and resume the *forward, march* when that section completes the wheel, so that they may not be too close during the display of the cross, and may move forward and keep the proper distance as soon as it is reduced.

The sections, in wheeling, form right angles with each other, and the alignment must be perfect.

If the Standard Guard is between either of these four sections, it obliques to the center as soon as the section in its front is about to commence the wheel, and quickly forms a close group, facing each other (inward), the Standard supported in the center by the three; it resumes its place in column when the same section begins the forward march.

If so instructed, the Standard Bearer may be detached, and, alone with the Standard, occupy the center of the cross; or the Select Commander may do so.

If there are eight sections (or threes), two crosses will be displayed at the same moment and in the same manner, the Vice-Commander filling the center of the leading cross, the Lieut.-Commander that of the one in the rear; the Standard Guard obliques to the center, between the two crosses, and halts. Or, the rear sections form square, triangle, etc., and reduce them as the cross is reduced. These combinations are numerous, and when well executed have a fine effect.

It is not so well, however, in the *display* as in the *formation* of Greek and other crosses.

The object in wheeling to the right is that the left guides may be on the marching flanks. If so instructed, the cross may be displayed to the left, and, in absence of the Standard Guard, the Select Commander with the Vice and Lieut.-Commanders, may place themselves in the center, back to back, thus:
∴. They resume their places in column as soon as the leading section commences the *forward march*.

To Form Greek Cross from Line.

1. *Form Greek Cross.* 2. MARCH. 3. *Forward.* 4. MARCH. 5. *Guide center.*

Four sections being in line, marching, with the Standard Guard in the center.

At the first command the officers command as follows:

Vice-Commander—1. *First section.* 2. *Threes left.*

Lieut.-Commander—1. *Fourth section.* 2. *To the rear.* 3. *Threes left.*

Chief of Standard Guard—1. *Center sections and Standard Guard.* 2. *Mark time.*

At the command MARCH, given as the right foot is coming to the ground, the first section wheels by threes, on movable pivots, to the left and marches in column of threes, parallel to the front of the second section, toward the center; the center sections and Standard Guard *mark time;* the fourth section executes *to the rear, march,* and immediately wheels by threes, on movable pivots, to the left, then marches in column of threes across the rear of the third section to the center. When the leading three of the first section reaches the front of the Standard Bearer, it executes *by the right flank,* forming column of files in front of the Standard; the second three advances and executes the same movement, from the same ground, the first section forming the upper limb of the cross, with the Vice-Commander at the top.

The leading (being the first) three of the fourth section forms column of files in rear of the Standard Bearer, by executing *by the left flank* and *marking time;* the second three of the fourth section *right obliques* to the rear of its first three and executes *by the left flank,* forming with it the lower limb of the cross, with the Lieut.-Commander in its rear. The Select Commander gives the fourth command, and the cross moves forward.

If so instructed, the flank sections may wheel by section and form the upper and lower parts of the cross without breaking by threes, and the commands of the Vice and Lieut.-Commanders are changed accordingly to, 1. *First section.* 2. *Left wheel*, etc.

Similar formations are made by double sections, threes, etc., to form Passion and other crosses, with or without the Standard Guard.

To Reduce Greek Cross to Line, Etc.

1. *Form line.* 2. MARCH. 3. *Forward.* 4. MARCH. 5. *Guide right* (or *left.*)

At the first command the Vice-Commander, placing himself on its right, commands: 1. *First section.* 2. *By the right flank.* Lieut.-Commander, placing himself on its left: 1. *Fourth section.* 2. *By the left flank.* Senior Workman: 1. *Center sections and Standard Guard.* 2. *Mark time.*

At the second command the first section executes *by the right flank*, forming line, and is conducted by the Vice-Commander to the right of the second section, caused to wheel on a movable pivot to the right, then executes *to the rear march*, and *marks time* in its place on the right of the line; in the mean time the lower limb of the cross (fourth section) executes *by the left flank*, is conducted by the Lieut.-Commander to the left of third section, and caused to *right wheel* (on a movable pivot) to its place on the left.

The Vice and Lieut.-Commanders take their places on the right and left as soon as their sections have gained their positions, and the Select Commander immediately commands, *forward*, etc.

If desired, the cross is reduced into column of sections, as before explained; or cross, formed from column of sections, may be reduced into line, as just explained. (See p. 136).

To Form Patriarchal Cross.

Being in column of threes.

1. *Form Patriarchal Cross.*   2. MARCH.   3. *Forward*
4. MARCH,   5. *Guide center.*

At the second command the first three executes *right forward, files right* and takes the short step, when its leading file has advanced two steps; the fourth, fifth and eighth threes execute the same movement and close upon the first three in column of files; the second three obliques to the right and marches forward, forming the right half of the horizontal limb of the cross, as explained for cross, with number one of the fourth three on its left; the third three obliques to the left, then marches forward, and with the second three and number one of the fourth three, forms the upper horizontal arms of the cross; the sixth three executes the movement as described for the second three, forming the right half (or arm) of the lower horizontal portion of the cross, with number three of the fifth three; the seventh three executes the movement described for the third three, forming in line with the sixth three and number three of the fifth three; the Vice and Lieut.-Commanders place themselves on the right and left flanks of the lower horizontal limbs, and the Select Commander places himself at the head of the cross and gives the fourth command.

[If the Standard Guard is present, the Standard Bearer quickly places himself in the center of one of the horizontal portins of the cross, the Jun. Work. and Sen. Work. taking the outer flanks, or moving with the Standard Bearer; the Vice and Lieut.-Commanders leading and following the column, and the Select Commander marches four yards from the left flank and abreast of the leading horizontal line. These various positions are determined by the number in ranks in order to preserve the proper proportions of the cross, and upon principles explained.]

Cross is formed from column of sections, etc., by similar commands and means.

To Reduce Patriarchal Cross.

1. *Form column.* 2. MARCH. 3. *Guide left.*

This is executed by means similar to the reduction of the Passion Cross, before explained.

To Form Cross of Salem.

Being in column of threes.

1. *Form Cross of Salem.* 2. MARCH. 3. *Guide center.*

Cross of Salem is a Patriarchal Cross, with an additional cross at its base, like the one at the top, and is formed by similar means; the rear cross forming, as has been explained for the upper part of Patriarchal Cross, closing up and uniting with the lower limb of the Patriarchal Cross.

The officers take their places, so as to effect the proper proportions of the different limbs of the cross, depending upon the number of threes (or sections) in the column.

To Reduce Cross of Salem.

1. *Form column.* 2. MARCH. 3. *Guide left.*

The cross is reduced by means similar to the reduction of other crosses, as before explained.

To Form Cross of St. Andrew from Column of Divisions or Double Sections.

1. *Form Cross of St. Andrew.* 2. *Left and right half wheel.* 3. MARCH. 4. *Right and left oblique.* 5. MARCH. 6. *Forward.* 7. MARCH. 8. *Guide center.*

At the second command the Vice-Commander commands:

1. *First division* [or *double section*, etc.] 2. *Left and right half wheel.*

Lieut.-Commander.—1. *Second division.* 2. *Right and left half wheel.*

At the command MARCH the leading division (half) wheels inwardly on fixed pivots, forming a letter V; the second division (half) wheels outwardly on movable pivots, forming an inverted Λ; the Standard Bearer retains his place, at the angle of the leading V, and the others of the Guard place themselves, abreast, twelve inches in his rear, and about six inches apart.

The Select Commander gives the fourth command in time to add MARCH the instant the half wheels are completed, at which the leading division faces to its former front and shortens the step a little; the second division faces in the same direction, and advancing obliquely toward the center, without deranging the positions of the shoulders, closes the interval between its leading files and the distance between them and the Standard Guard, so as to form the letter X with the Standard Bearer is in its center. The Vice and Lieut.-Commanders quickly place themselves, in echelon, at the heads of the cross (the Vice on the right) which marches with full step to its present front, late front of the column, at command of the Select Commander, who places himself in front of the Standard and on a line with the Vice and Lieut.-Commanders.

If there be no Standard Guard, the Select Commander occupies the center, and the Vice and Lieut.-Commanders take position as described for the guard.

To Reduce Cross of St. Andrew.

1. *Form column.* 2. *Right and left front into line.* 3 MARCH. 4. *Guide left.*

At the second command the officers quickly place themselves in front of the several arms of the cross and command:

Vice-Commander—(To upper right arm). 1. *First section.* 2. *Left front into line.*

Lieut. Commander—(To lower left arm). 1. *Fourth section.*
2. *Left front into line.*
Sen. Work.—(To lower right arm). 1. *Third section.*
2. *Right front into line.*
Jun. Work.—(To upper left arm). 1. *Second section.*
2. *Mark time.*

[If the arms of the cross are more or less than a section, change the command to suit, thus: "*Right wing, first division. Left front into line,*" etc.]

At the command MARCH the several sections of the cross execute the commands, and the leading section, having formed line, marches forward at command of the Vice-Commander; as soon as the second section is unmasked it executes *right front into line* at command of the Jun. Work., and by his command obliques into its place in column. The other sections are marched into their places by similar commands and means, regulating the step so as to immediately gain their position in column, and the officers take their places.

TRIANGLES.

From Column of Files.

Station two markers two yards apart, opposite each other, near the apex, and one at each angle at the base of triangle to be formed. The column being in march, command:

1. *Form triangle.* 2. *Column half left and right.*
3. MARCH.

The third command is given when the column is about three yards from the markers at the apex.

The Vice-Commander conducts the column *half left*, parallel to the line of the markers on that side, halts his division when its head has reached the point opposite the place where it will rest, and faces it to the right; the Sen. Work. follows, conducting his center division until nearing the point where the first division inclined to the left, when he marches it *column half left*, in rear of the first division beyond the marker at the angle at the base, marches it.*column right* three yards in rear of and opposite the base of the triangle, halts and faces it to the right; the Lieut.-Commander follows, with the third division, to the ground from which the first division changed direction, then by *column half right* marches it parallel to the line of markers on that side, halts it opposite its place, and causes it to *left face*.

Each chief, having faced his division toward the center, as soon as it arrives opposite its place, places himself at his proper angle against the marker, and dresses his division up to the line toward himself, leaving room for the Commander to form the apex, with the Chaplain inside the triangle.

The Jun. Work. hastens to place himself in front of the second division, when it first changes direction, near the apex of the triangle

To Reduce the Triangle.

1. *Column of files.* 2. *Right and left.* 3. Face.
4. *Forward.* 5. March.

At the second command the Vice-Commander and Jun. Work. command: 1. —*division*. 2. *Right*, the Lieut.-Commander. 1. *Third division*. 2. *Left*, and the chiefs repeat the third command. At the command *forward*, the Vice-Commander commands: 1. *First division*. 2. *Stand fast*. At March the Lieut.-Commander conducts his division back, left in front, over the ground it traversed in forming the triangle; the Sen. Work. conducts the second division past the rear of the first division, retracing its steps to the point where it executed *column half left*, and there unites in column of files with and in rear of the Lieut.-Commander's division, and resumes his own place (the Jun. Work. takes his place as soon as the second division commences the *forward march*); the Vice-Commander causes his division to move forward in rear of and uniting with the second division as it passes, and takes his place in rear of the column.

When the divisions are joined in column of files, the Select Commander halts and faces it to the right, continues the march, left in front, or he commands *to the rear*, MARCH, or uses such other method to bring the right in front as he desires.

To Form Triangle from Column of Threes about a Grave or Delta.

1. *Form triangle.* 2. *Column half right and left.* 3. MARCH.

If the Standard Guard occupies the center of the column, the Sen. Work. and Jun. Work. immediately place themselves in front and rear of the center column, and at the command MARCH, the two left columns march together, *column half left*, and the right division marches *column half right*, conducted by their chiefs to their places, as before.

To Reduce the Triangle.

1. *Column of threes.* 2. *Right and left.* 3. FACE. 4. *Forward.* 5. MARCH.

The divisions step off together, retrace their steps, conducted by their chiefs, and each is halted when its rear reaches the ground from which it changed direction at the apex of the triangle to march out of column. The Jun. Work. takes his place in the second division as soon as it commences the *forward march;* the chiefs of divisions resume their places as the column is re-formed.

If it be desired to form column of files, the commands are given as before explained, and the movement is similarly executed.

To Form Triangle from Column of Threes.

Being in march.

1. *To half distance, close column.* 2. MARCH.

Executed as before explained.

1. *Form triangle.* 2. MARCH.

At the first command the Jun. Work. hastens to place himself in rear of the rear file of the middle column; the Vice-

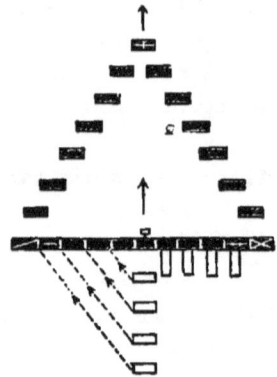

Commander, passing by the right to rear, commands: 1. *Files.* 2. *Right into echelon.* The Lieut.-Commander, stepping to the left of the column, commands: 1. *Files.* 2. *Left into echelon,* and both Vice and Lieut.-Commanders quickly go to the rear of their column; the Senior Workman, without moving from his place, commands: 1. *Center file.* 2 *Mark time.*

At the command MARCH, the center column of files *marks time;* the leading files of the right and left column shorten the step. When these columns have passed about half their length, the Senior Work. commands: 1. *Center column.* 2. *Forward.* 3. *Column right.* 4. MARCH, which it executes; and the Senior Work. immediately commands: 1. *By the left flank.* 2. *Rear files.* 3. *Left front into line;* adding 4. MARCH the instant before the Standard Bearer would have turned to the right.

The Select Knights, who have changed direction to the right, face to the left and advance in line by short steps: the rear files execute *left front into line;* the Senior Work. quickly takes his place on the right of his division; the Vice- and Lieut.-Commanders form the last files of their respective divisions; the rear division, when formed, closes up on the other two with the full step, and the Select Commander commands: 1. *Forward.* 2. MARCH. 3. *Guide center,* and places himself in front of the leading files, thus completing the triangle.

The triangle may be formed at open order (threes distance) if desired, by omitting the command for closing to half distance.

The center column may form the base of the triangle by wheeling around the Standard, as before described for similar movement, or the Standard Guard may occupy the center of the triangle, if so instructed.

To Reduce Triangle.

1. *Column of threes.* 2. *Mark time.* 3. MARCH.

At the first command the Vice and Lieut.-Commanders command their respective divisions to *mark time;* the Sen. Work. steps in front of his division, and commands: 1.*Right wing.* 2. *Left wheel,* and the Jun. Work., facing the left wing of the second division, commands: 1. *Left wing.* 2. *To the rear.* 3. *Left wheel.* At the command MARCH the right and left divisions and the Standard Bearer *mark time;* the half of the second division, which is at the right of the Standard Bearer, wheels to the left, describing a quarter circle about him; the left half of the division executes *to the rear, march,* and immediately commences the left wheel, similar to the movement of the right wing. The Sen. Work. commands: 1. *From right take distance by right and left flanks,* and adds MARCH the instant the wings have wheeled perpendicu- to their late line, when both wings face toward the apex of the triangle, and, except the leading file, halts; the leading file marches forward, and each Select Knight in succession resumes the *forward march* at the distance of fifty-four inches from the one in front.

Seeing that the head of the center column is nearly up to its place, the Commander commands: 1. *Form threes.* 2. MARCH. The Sen. Work. and Jun. Work. quickly take their places on the right and left of the Standard Bearer, and Select Knights in the outer columns face and march directly to their places in column of threes; the Vice and Lieut.-Commander take their posts at the head and rear of the column. The Commander commands: *Forward* MARCH at the proper time.

Threes in Triangles.

Being in column of threes, at section distance.

1. *Threes in triangles.* 2. MARCH.

At the command MARCH, given as the right foot strikes the

ground, numbers one and three of each three *mark time* and numbers two take two short steps, and then all resume the full step.

If in column of threes, at wheeling distance, it is executed as described, the leading three marching forward on the third step, and the others *halt;* each three in succession marching forward, at caution of its chief, when it has gained section distance from the three in its front.

The Vice and Lieut.-Commanders lead and follow the column at half distance (54 inches).

The Standard Guard forms triangle as other threes.

1. *Form threes.* 2. MARCH.

At MARCH, the Select Knight forming the apex of each triangle marks time, the others advance by the short step, and the threes, united, march forward.

To Form Triangle from Column of Sections.

Being closed to half distance.

1. *Form triangle.* 2. *Threes half right and left.* 3. MARCH.

At the second command the chief of third section commands *forward;* the right three of the leading section wheels, on a movable pivot, *half right*, and upon completion of the wheel of one-eighth of a circle, each Select Knight faces to the late front, and by oblique steps, shoulders square to the front, close the apex of the triangle (to within twelve inches) with the left three, which executes the same movements to the left, and both *mark time;* the right and left threes of the second section wheel as described, advance obliquely, and unite in echelon with the threes of the first section, at the caution of their chiefs; the Vice and Lieut.-Commanders take their places in echelon at the rear; the third section marches forward (breaking in the center sufficient to admit the Standard Bearer, who halts when the movement is commenced), and the Sen. Work. and Jun. Work. place themselves on the flanks at the base of the triangle. The Commander forms its apex in front. The length of the steps and acuteness of the angles necessary will be seen and readily determined on once executing the movement.

If there are more than three sections, those in rear form a second triangle, a cross, square, etc., as may be indicated by the commands and as they may have been before instructed. *Double sections* may be formed into triangle by similar means, the commands being: 1. *Form triangle.* 2. *Sections right and left half wheel*, etc.

To Re-form Column of Sections.

1. *Form sections.* 2. MARCH. 3. *Guide center.*

At the command MARCH the Vice-Commander takes his place at the head of the column; the leading Select Knights take the short step while the others of the first section march forward to their places, and the section takes the twenty-eight inch step; the threes of the second section march obliquely toward each other, unite, face to the front, re-form the section as just described, and march forward when at section distance; the rear section marks time, until it gains its place in column, and marches forward; the Treasurer and other officers promptly take their proper places by the shortest line.

To Form Square from Column of Sections.

Being in march.

1. *Form square.* 2. MARCH. 3. *Forward.* 4. MARCH.

At the first command the chiefs of sections command as follows, viz.:

1st section, *Mark time.* 2d and 3d sections, 1. *Right and left forward.* 2. *Files right and left.* 4th section and Standard Guard, *Forward.*

At the second command the first section *marks time;* the right threes of the second and third sections execute the *right forward, files right,* and close in column of files on the chief of first section and *mark time;* the left threes of the same sections execute the *left forward, files left*, closing up and 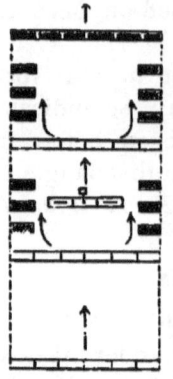 marking time in rear on the left guide of section one ; the Standard Guard marches forward to the middle of the square, and the Commander gives the fourth command the instant the fourth section closes the square in rear. The Commander and Lieut.-Commander dart into the square as it is forming and form a line in front of the Standard Guard, the Commander on the right, the Lieut.-Commander on the left; or, if so instructed, the Vice and Lieut.-Commanders may place themselves on the flanks of the first section, and the Sen. Work. and Jun. Work. place themselves on the flank of the rear section (to increase the front); the sides of the square will oblique so as to cover the Vice and Lieut.-Commanders instead of the chief and guide of the leading section; the Commander and Standard only occupying the center, or the Standard alone doing so.

Formation of square from double sections is similarly executed, and the officers, with the Standard Guard, form line, double rank, or triangle within the square. Any odd sections in rear form as the Commander shall indicate by commands, thus: 1. *Form square.* 2. *Rear sections form triangle,* etc., and are formed and reduced as explained. This applies to nearly all the formations of like character.

To Reduce Square.

1. *Column of sections.* 2. *Right and left front into line.* 3. MARCH. 4. *Guide* LEFT.

At the first command the Vice-Commander, approaching near to the right side of the square, commands, in a low tone, *Left front into sections;* the Lieut.-Commander approaches near to the left side of the square and commands, in a low tone, *Right front into sections;* the chief of the fourth section, *mark time*. At the command *march* the first section moves forward; the second and third sections are re-formed as indicated by the commands, until each in succession has gained section distance, when, at command of their chiefs, they take the full step forward, and so with section four. The officers immediately resume their proper posts; the Standard Guard regulates its steps so as to regain its place as soon as the second section advances.

To Reduce Greek Cross to the Left.

1. *Form column to the left.*   2. MARCH.   3. *Guide left.*

See page 118.

At the first command the Vice-Commander orders: *First section by the left flank;* the chief of second section commands, *left wheel;* the chief of the third 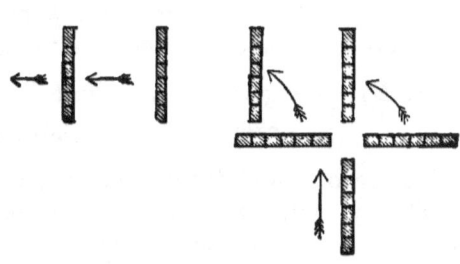 section, and Lieut.-Commander cautions the third and fourth sections that they will have to *mark time*. The command *march* is given as the left foot strikes the ground, when the first section marches by the left flank; the second section wheels on a movable pivot to the left and follows the first. As the second section is about to pass in front of the third section its chief commands: 1. *Third section.*   2. *Left wheel.*   2. MARCH; when it wheels into its place in column. The Lieut.-Commander orders, 1. *Fourth section.*   2. *Forward.*   3. MARCH, and when it reaches the rear of the column, commands 1. *By the left flank.*   2. MARCH.

Or, square may be formed from Greek Cross thus:

1. *Form square.*   2. MARCH.

At the first command chiefs of double section (or sections) command:

1st and 4th double sections—1. *By the left flank.* 2. *Right wheel.*

2nd and 3rd double sections—*Left wheel.*

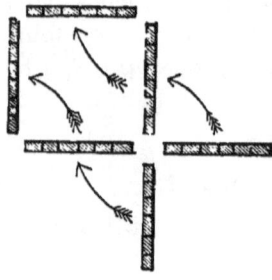

At the command *march*, the double sections wheel as indicated by the commands; the double sections regulating their steps so that they will not interfere with others, and each completes its wheel as nearly as possible at the same instant. The Commander, Vice and Lieut.-Commanders place themselves within the square as before explained, and the Commander orders:

   1. *By the right* (or *left*) *flank.* 2. *Square forward.*
            3. MARCH. 4. *Guide center.*

The second and third subdivisions execute *by the right flank*, and with the rear subdivision close to their places in the square, and move forward.

   1. *Form column.* 2. MARCH. 3. *Guide left.*

At the second command chiefs of subdivisions see that their subdivisions gain their places in column by these movements. 1st. Subdivision—*Forward;* executed by shortening the steps a little. 2nd. 1. *By the left flank.* 2. *Right wheel,* following in trace of the leading subdivision at subdivision distance.

3rd and 4th Subdivisions—1. ———. 2. *Mark time.*

3rd Subdivision executes, 1. *Forward.* 2. *Column right.* 3. MARCH, and having gained its place in column. 1. *By the left flank.* 2. MARCH.

4th Subdivision. 1. *Forward.* 2. MARCH. when the 3rd subdivision is at proper distance.

The Commander orders *Guide Left* when the command *march* is given to the rear subdivision, and the full step is taken.

Or the cross may be re-formed thus:

    1. *Form Greek Cross..*   2. MARCH.

The first subdivisions execute the following movements:

1st and 4th subdivisions—*Left wheel,* then *by the right flank.*

2nd and 3rd subdivisions—*Right wheel,* and seeing the movements completed the cross marches forward by the usual commands and means.

These hints are deemed sufficient for the execution of the movement.

To Form Initial Letters From Column of Sections.

    1. *Form initial letters.*   2. MARCH.   3. *Forward.*
    4. MARCH.   5. *Guide left.*

At the second command the first section stands fast (or halts, if the column is in march) and the Vice-Commander hastens to place himself in rear of its center; the right three of the second section executes *right forward, files right,* and forms a column of files with the Knight on the right of the first section; the left three executes *left forward, files left,* closing in a similar manner on the left guide of the first section—thus forming the letter **E**; the third section continues the march and halts at full threes distance from

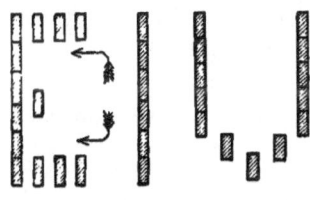

the rear files of the second section; the fourth section closes to half distance, on the third, its left file promptly taking his place (in echelon) so that his right shoulder will be twelve inches in rear of the left shoulder of number two, of his three; the Lieut.-Commander quickly places himself in the same relative position with the left file of the section, (or so that his right shoulder is twelve inches in rear of the left shoulder of number three of the second three of the fourth section); the left guide of the fifth section lengthens his steps, inclining slightly to the right and places himself in echelon with the Lieut.-Commander so that his left shoulder shall be twelve inches in rear of the right shoulder of the Lieut.-Commander, and the section closes up so its left file (number two) shall cover the right shoulder of number three with his left, as described for the others who are in echelon. Each section haults when it gains its position.

The third section, in line, forms the letter I; the fourth and fifth, with the Lieut.-Commander, the letter U.

If the Standard Guard is in column, the distance between the initial letters is section distance (and may be so in its absence, if so instructed). The Standard Bearer marches between the threes of the second section, breaks, and takes the Vice-Commander's place, who takes his position as a "full stop" midway between the letters E and I. The Junior Workman quickly takes the place described for the Lieut.-Commander, who will form the "period" for the letter U, and the Senior Workman forms the period between the I and U.

The column moves forward and may march by the flank by the usual commands, and means.

To Reduce Inital Letters To Column.

1. *Form column.* 2. MARCH.

At the command *march* the officers and odd files resume their places in column of sections; the first section moves forward; the threes of the second re-forms the section by executing *left* and *right front into line;* each section takes up the march on gaining its distance.

To Form Diamond.

1. *Form diamond.* 2. MARCH. 3. *Forward.* 4. MARCH. 5. *Guide center.*

At the second command the leading section makes a three-quarter wheel to the left, on a fixed pivot; the second advances

LEGION AND DISPLAY DRIL 139

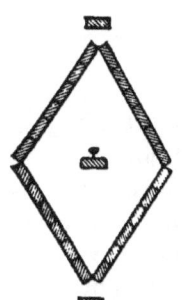
to near the ground from which the first commenced the movement, and makes a three-quarter wheel to the right on a movable pivot, its guide directing his movement so that he shall gradually approach the right of the first section; the third section obliques to the left about half its front, advances to within a little less than section distance of the rear of the first section, and wheels to the right, so that its left will join the left of the first section; the fourth section obliques to the right about half its front, advances to the right of the third section, wheels to the left so as to close the diamond; each section halts and faces to its former front on arriving in its place; the Vice-Commander places himself, faced to rear, twelve inches in front of the point where the right of the first and left of the second sections will rest, and aids the Commander in superintending and directing the formation, who places himself in the center and on a line with the opposite flanks of the sections; the Lieut.-Commander quickly places himself in front of the Vice-Commander, on a line with the chief and twelve inches in rear of the point where the right of the third and left of the fourth sections will rest, aiding in directing the movements. At the third command the Vice-commander faces about; and the diamond marches toward the former front of the column at the fourth command.

To Reduce Diamond.

1. *Form Column.* 2. MARCH.

At the command *march* the several sections form into sections by *left* (and *right*) *front into line;* the first section marches forward and the others oblique into their places at command of their chiefs.

School of the Battalion.

NO manual or drill for a battalion of select Knights has heretofore been published; yet uniformity and precision of movement, certainty as to the commands and the particular thing to be done, or that is required of the officers and Legions, are essential in public parades.

A battalion of Select Knights is composed of two or more Legions, not exceeding eight. In emergencies the number may be increased, but it is better for the Legions to be consolidated and equalized, or formed in two or more battalions.

Independent Legions, of marked difference in size, formed into column, with bands at irregular distances, detract very much from the beauty that whould be the result of a more systematic formation.

The first important thing is promptness. This cannot be too strongly emphasized.

The details of this drill are given as full as the limit of space admits.

In describing the movements, "at one" is sometimes used to indicate the first command; "at two" for the second command, and so on. Plain abbreviations are also used.

Who Commands.

"When Legions appear in public, in their own State or out of it, they are under the immediate authority of the Grand Commander, if he choses to assume the command.

If he is not present, an officer upon whom under the constitution his duties devolve may act in his place. But all are under the authority of the Grand Commander in whose juridiction they may at the time be."

An officer properly in command, and present, may detail any Select Knight under him to assist or to give the oral commands; but it would be courteous first to obtain the acquiescence of the next in rank.

The Grand Commander is recognized, in this work, as the chief in command of battalion.

If he divides his command into two or more battalions, the Grand Officers, according to rank, should command them, the Grand Commander directing the several movements.

The Grand Vice-Commander is second in command. There is no such office as adjutant known to the law of Select Knights; it is therefore appropriate for the Grand Recorder to perform the duties of adjutant when occasion requires such an officer.

It may be remarked *en passant* that, for similar reasons, and that his duties are somewhat assimilated thereto, the Treasurer might be utilized as Quarter Master when Select Knights go into camp or on excursions.

When Commands are Repeated and Executed.

Officers in command of wings repeat commands whenever necessary; chiefs of Legions repeat those, different from the others, which are to be immediately executed by their Legions. In successive movements each chief of Legion gives the command necessary to insure the execution of the movement by his Legion at the proper time. Commands are executed on hearing them from the Grand Commander.

Rank and Position of Legions.

Legions—Grand and Subordinate—take rank according to the dates of their several organizations, unless they voluntarily waive their proper rank.

They form in order of rank from right to left, and in battalion movements are designated, numerically, from right to left when in line, and from front to rear when in column, as *first Legion*, *second Legion*, and so on.

A SQUADRON is properly two mounted Legions, but the nomenclature of the order forces the use of *division* (in U. S. infantry battalion drill, two companies) in the sense of a military platoon; hence we use *squadron* to indicate two Legions in the Select Knights' battalion drill, if more than two are present, whether mounted or on foot.

In column of squadrons, Legion are designated from the head of the column, and from right to left of each squadron, as *first Legion, second Legion first squadron,* and so on.

The numbers of Legions and squadrons change when, by facing in the opposite direction, the left becomes the right of the line, and the rear the head of the column. If in passing from line into column, or the reverse, the designation is changed; they hold their last designation until the movement is completed, when the chiefs immediately caution; (such) *Legion;* so with the squadrons.

The ranking officer of the squadron commands it in column of squadrons, having regard to the rank of the officer himself, as well as his Legion (unless he waive his right).

FOR PRACTICE DRILL large Legions can treat double sections, or sections as Legions, placing the best drilled Select Knights in command.

Equalization of Legions.

In drill it is important that the Legions should be equal. Large Legions may, for this purpose, be divided into two or more, one of which occupies its place according to rank, and the others on its left according to the direction of the Commander. Small Legions might be consolidated and take rank from the oldest Legion, in the consolidation, according to the equities of the case. That is, if a senior Legion, taking the right, had one or more supernumeraries, it would not be just for these to be consolidated with the junior Legion so as to give it fictitious rank.

The Standards.

Unless every Legion has its Standard and guard, those

SCHOOL OF THE BATTALION.

present could be grouped and form a Battalion Standard Guard, which occupies the center of the battalion, with the Grand Standard Guard on its right. Its chief is the Grand Senior Workman, on its right, unless its number (always the multiple of three) exceed six, when its chief may be detached, the same as a chief of Legion.

Its numerical strength never exceeds that of the Legions. It would doubtless prove satisfactory for the Standard Bearer, as left file of the right center division of each Legion, to carry a light banner with the "coat of arms" of his Legion emblazoned upon it.

When the Grand Standard Bearer is referred to in this drill, it will be understood as the Standard Bearer nearest the center of the battalion.

When chiefs of Legions are referred to, the term applies as well, generally, to the chief of the Battalion Standard Guard.

Post of Officers.

The Grand Commander, Grand Vice-Commander and Grand Lieut.-Commander are (supposed to be) mounted, and will be called *Field Officers*.

The Grand Commander is posted in front of the center of the line at a distance equal to about half its front, not exceeding thirty yards. He goes wherever his presence is necessary.

*Gr. Com.

Gr. Lt. Com.*   *G. V. C.

Chiefs of L.   *   *   *   *   *   *
Gr. J.W.*——— ——— ——— ———†——— ——— ——— ———*Gr. S.W.

The Vice-Grand Commander and *Grand Lieut.-Commanders* are on a line in front of the centers of the right and left wings, at a distance equal to about half the front of the wing.

The Grand Senior Workman and Grand Junior Workman, in maneuvers of the battalion, may act as Adjutant and Sergeant-Major respectively, and also as right and left general guides; they are posted on the right and left of the battalion, except when acting as Adjutant and Sergeant-Major, when they are three yards from the flanks, and aid the Gr. Vice-Commander and Gr. Lieut.-Commander.

Officers in charge of Legions, and the chief of the Battalion Standard Guard, if he is not a part of the Guard itself, are two yards in front of the center of their respective commands.

The Markers

Should, if practicable, be Knights temporarily detached from the Battalion Standard Guard or flank Legions, and their intervals left for them; otherwise they retire, after the line is formed, behind the flanks of the battalion Standard Guard [abbreviated Bat. St. Gd.]; or, in maneuvers, are one yard in rear of the right and left flanks of flank battalion Legions in line or the same distance from the leading and rear subdivisions on the opposite side from the guide, in column.

To Form the Battalion.

The Legions form on their parade grounds at the sound of the *assembly* [in army, at *adjutant's call*], and the Grand Senior and Junior Workmen, each covered by a marker, march to the battalion parade ground, when each posts a marker, facing the other, at a distance apart a little less than the front of a Legion, each standing three yards in rear of the marker nearest to him, the Grand Senior Workman being toward the right of the line. The Grand Senior Workman then takes a side step to the left, the Grand Junior Workman to the right, draw swords, face about, and each proceeds, Legion distance, toward the right and left of the line, when they halt and face about, and again cover the markers. The line is prolonged in the right wing by the Vice-Commanders (as right guides), who precede their Legions, on the line by about fifteen yards and establish themselves, facing the markers, each at Legion distance from the marker in front of him. The Grand Senior Workman assures the position of the right guides, placing himself in their rear (as before described), as they successively arrive. The line is similarly prolonged in the left wing by the Lieut-Commanders as left guides, the Grand Junior Workman assuring their position as they successively arrive.

The guides invert their swords in front of the center of the body, cross-hilt above the head, flat of the blade next to them.

The Battalion Standard Guard is the first established, and is conducted by its chief so as to arrive from the rear, parallel with the markers. When it arrives in rear of the line it is halted, and its chief, placing himself, facing to the front, near the left marker, dresses the guard to the left—[or if there is no Battalion Standard Guard, then the right center Legion is so dressed by its chief] the breasts of Select Knights opposite the markers resting against their arms. The Legions of the right wing form successively from left to right, each being halted three yards from the line and dressed to the left, as explained for the Battalion Standard Guard. The Legions of the left wing form successively from right to left, and are dressed to the right. In alignments the Vice and Lieut.-Commanders on the flank toward which the alignment is made, if not employed to mark the line, step back to enable the chiefs of Legions to align their Legions.

Each chief commands: 1. (such) *Legion.* 2. *Support.* 3. SWORDS, as soon as the chief next succeeding him in his own wing commands *front*; the flank Legions *support swords* as soon as dressed.

THE BAND forms (at the place designated by the acting adjutant) at the sound of the *assembly of musicians*, which precedes the *assembly*, and marches at the same time with the Legions, playing in quick time to its position in line.

The Field Officers take their places, the Grand Commander only facing the line.

The Grand Senior Workman, having assured the position of the Vice-Commanders of the right Legions, faces about, marches three yards to the right of the front rank, faces to the left, moves two yards to the front, halts and faces to the left, and when the last Legion arriving on the line is brought to *support swords*, commands: 1. *Guides*. 2. Posts.

At this command the Grand Junior Workman, chiefs of Legions, Vice and Lieut.-Commanders and markers take their posts in line; the markers passing through the intervals, made by the Vice and Lieut.-Commanders near them, stepping one yard to the front, who then resume their places; the Grand Junior Workman takes his position on the left flank.

The chief of Battalion Standard Guard occupies the same relative position, if not forming a part of the guard itself, and is included when chiefs of Legions are referred to.

The Grand Senior Workman then passes along the front, in rear of the chiefs of Legions, to the center, turns to the right, halts midway between the chiefs of Legions and the Grand Commander, faces about, brings the battalion to a *carry* and *present swords* (which the Gr. C. acknowledges by raising chapeau) resumes his front, salutes the Grand Commander, and reports: *Sir, the battalion is formed.*

The Grand Commander returns the salute with the right hand, directs the Grand Senior Workman to *take your post, Sir Knight*, draws his sword and commands: 1. *Carry*. 2. Swords.

The Grand Senior Workman faces about, retraces his steps, and takes position on the right flank.

To Open Ranks.

Being at a halt.

1. *Rear open order*. 2. March.

At the first command the Grand Senior Workman places himself three yards in rear of the right flank, facing to the left; the Grand Junior Workmen places himself three yards in rear of the left of the left flank, faces toward the right, and inverts his sword; the Vice-Commanders of the right, and Lieut.-Commanders of the left Legions, step back three yards opposite their places in line to mark the new alignment of the rear rank; they are aligned by the Grand Vice-Commander on the Grand Junior Workman who inverts his sword.

At the command MARCH the front rank dresses to the right and the rear rank steps to the rear, passes a little in rear of the established line and dresses forward on the Vice Commanders, who verify the alignments of their respective Legions.

The chiefs of Legions place themselves three yards in front of the center of their Legions, dress to the right and cast their eyes to the front as soon as their alignment is verified.

The Grand Commander superintends the alignment of the Legion officers and front rank, and the Grand Vice and Lieut.-Commanders the rear rank.

At the command *front*, the Grand Vice and Lieut.-Commanders take their places, and the Vice and Lieut.-Commanders place themselves on the line of the chiefs of Legion in front of the centers of the right and left wings of their Legions; the Grand Senior and Junior Workmen step straight to the front and dress on a line of Legion officers; the Grand Commander, passing to the center in front of the line of Legion officers, places himself, facing to the front, six yards in advance of the line of the Grand Vice and Lieut.-Commanders.

To Close the Ranks.

1. *Close order*, 2. MARCH.

At the second command the officers face about and return to their places in line; the rear rank closes to facing distance.

To Open Order in Single Rank.

The same rules and commands apply, except that numbers two step to the rear, as before explained (School of the Legion).

At the command, 1. *Close order*. 2. MARCH, the rear rank resumes its place in the front rank, and the movement is completed as before.

To Dismiss the Battalion.

Dismiss your Legions. At this order each chief of Legion marches his Legion to its parade ground, where it is dismissed.

To March in Line.

1. *Forward*. 2. *Guide center*. 3. MARCH.

At the second command the right and left general guides (Grand Senior and Junior Workmen, advance six yards to the front; the Standard Bearer of the center Legion (or Grand Standard Bearer, or Standard Bearer of the senior Legion if there be a Battalion Standard Guard) advances abreast of the Grand Senior and Junior Workmen, the Commander of the Battalion Standard Guard takes his place in the line. The chiefs of Legions place themselves in the front rank on the right of their Legions, and the Senior Workmen step back two yards straight to the rear; or, if there are two ranks, step back into the rear rank and cover their chiefs.

The Battalion Standard Guard forms the basis of the alignment, its chief following in trace of the standard in its front. If there be no Battalion Standard Guard, the right center Legion is the basis of the alignment. The chiefs of Legions occasionally turn their heads slightly toward the basis of alignment (shoulders square to the front) in order to maintain themselves on the same line, each regaining his position, if lost, by almost insensible degrees.

The Grand Vice-Commander and Grand Lieut.-Commander place themselves in rear of the battalion, opposite their places in line, and superintend the march of the right and left wings, from the rear of their centers; Grand Senior and Junior Workmen three yards in rear to assist.

Similar rules govern the battalion movements as are prescribed for Legions.

To Face the Battalion to the Rear and March it to the Rear.

Being in line.
1. *Threes right* (or *left*) *about.* 2. MARCH. 3. *Battalion.* 4. HALT. Or, 3. *Guide center.*

At one, the Grand Standard Bearer and general guides, if not already there, return to their places in line; the battalion wheels about by threes at the second command. If halted, the chiefs of Legions, placing themselves on the flanks of their Legions toward the center, dress them in that direction; the Guide or Lieut.-Commanders on that flank step to the rear. In wheeling about by threes, when marching in line, each chief of Legion describes a semi-circle, whose radius is twenty-two inches, and thus places himself on the flank of his Legion, according as before the movement he was on its right or left.

If the march be continued, after wheeling about by threes, at the command *Guide center*, the Grand Standard Bearer and general guides advance six yards in front of the line and assume the direction of the march; the chiefs of Legions, if not already there, place themselves on the flanks of their Legions farthest from the Standard

When a battalion in line wheels about by threes, the Field Officers, unless otherwise directed, place themselves in rear by passing around its flanks. The battalion is then maneuvered by the same commands and means as when facing in the opposite direction.

To march the battalion a few yards to the rear, command:
1. *Battalion..* 2. ABOUT. 3. FACE. 4. *Forward.* 5. *Guide center* 6. MARCH.

Or, if in march, commmand:
1. *To the rear.* 2. MARCH. 3. *Guide center.*

Officers retain their relative positions until it is again faced to the front.

School of the Battalion.

To Oblique in Line and Resume the Forward.

1. *Right* (or *left*) *oblique.* 2. MARCH.

Executed as before explained.

To resume the direct march: 1. *Forward.* 2. MARCH.

To Halt the Battalion.

1. *Battalion.* 2. HALT.

If the direct march is not to be resumed.

1. *Standard and general guides.* 2. POSTS.

The order is obeyed, and chiefs of Legions resume their places in front as the guides step into their intervals.

To Rectify an Alignment.

Commanders rectify the alignment.

The chiefs of Legions place themselves on the flanks of their Legions toward the Standard (the guides, or files, stepping to the rear) and successively dressing toward the center, when the preceding chief commands *front.* Each returning to his place in line after commanding *front.*

To Give General Alignment.

The Grand Commander places himself outside one flank of the battalion and commands:

1. *Standard and general guides on the line.* 2. *Guides on the line.* 3. *Center.* 4. DRESS. 5. *Standard and guides.* 6. POSTS.

At one, the Grand Standard Bearer and general guides place themselves on the line and face to the Grand Commander, who establishes them by motion of the sword in the direction he wishes to give the battalion.

At two, the Vice-Commanders of Legions to the right of the Grand Standard and Lieut.-Commanders of Legions to the left, face toward the Standard, and each places himself at Legion distance in rear of the next one before him, and aligns himself on the Standard Bearer and the general guides beyond.

The chiefs of the Legions hasten to place themselves on the flanks of their Legions toward the Standard, and the guide on that flank quickly passes by the rear and occupies the interval left by the guide on the line.

The left file of Battalion Standard Guard places himself in the interval left by the Grand Standard Bearer, and the chief occupies the interval so made for him.

The Field Officers on the right and left wings place themselves outside the general guides and assure the position of the guides in their own wings.

At four, the Legions move up in quick time against the guides, and each chief of Legion commands: 1. *Left* (or *right*) 2. DRESS. 3. FRONT, according as he is on the right or left of the Standard.

If the new line be oblique and at considerable distance from the battalion, the chiefs of Legions conduct their commands so as to arrive parallel to their places in line, then dress, as before explained.

At the sixth command the officers and guides resume their places in line. If the new direction of line be such that Legions find themselves in advance, the Grand Commander, before establishing guides, causes these Legions to move to the rear.

To Change Direction in Line.

1. *Battalion.* 2. *Right* (or *left*) *wheel.* 3. MARCH.

At two, the Grand Standard Bearer and general guides place themselves six yards in front, as before explained; the chiefs of Legions place themselves on the flanks of their Legions farthest from the Battalion Standard Guard; the field officer of the left wing places himself on the left of the left general guide, and the field officer of the right wing on the right of the front rank.

At the command MARCH, the chief of the right Legion

SCHOOL OF THE BATTALION.

stands fast, or, halts, and is the pivot; the left general guide takes the full step, wheels as if on the marching flank; the chief of left Legion follows in his trace, preserving distance; the Grand Standard Bearer preserves his distance on the line with left general guide and pivot, or slightly in rear of it.

The field officers superintend the movements of the general guide and wing nearest them.

1. *Battalion*. 2. HALT. Or, 1. *Forward*. 2. MARCH. 3. *Guide center*, is given when wheeled sufficiently.

At *forward* the Grand Standard Bearer advances to the line of the general guides. At the second command resume the direct step; the field officers return to their posts.

To March by the Flank, from Line.

1. *Threes right* (or *left*). 2. MARCH.

The Grand Commander marches on the side of the guide about thirty yards from the center of the column. The Grand Vice-Commander and Grand Lieut.-Commander on the same side, about six yards from the head or rear of the column, each in his own wing, the general guides between them and the column.

In all movements on the march, from the order in line to the order in column, the Grand Standard Bearer, at the preparatory command, resumes his position in line.

The battalion may be faced to the right or left from line and marched forward, or marched by the flanks by the usual commands for a Legion.

To Break into Column of Threes from the Right or Left, to March to the Left or Right.

Being in line at a halt.

1. *Column of Threes*. 2. *Break from the right* (or *left*) *to march to the left* (or *right*). 3. MARCH.

At two, the chief of the right Legion orders: 1. *Right forward*. 2. *Threes right*.

At the command MARCH, repeated by the chief, the Legion moves in column of threes to the front; the chief

commanding. 1. *Column left*, adding 2. MARCH, the instant
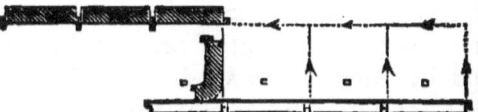 the leading three
has advanced Legion
distance; the guard
then directs his march
parallel with the front of the battalion. The chief of the
second Legion orders: 1. *Right forward.* 2. *Threes right*,
adding 3. MARCH when the leading guide of the first Legion
arrives opposite his right three; the Legion advances and
changes direction as explained for the first Legion, following
in its rear.

The other Legions successively conform to what is
explained for the second.

Being in column of threes, the battalion is halted, put in
march, obliques, changes direction, marches to the rear, forms
files, sections or divisions, etc., the same as a Legion, substituting *battalion* for *Legion*.

To Form Line to the Right or Left from Column of Threes.

1. *Threes right* (or *left*). 2. MARCH. 3. *Battalion.*
4. HALT. Or, 3. *Guide center.*

The HALT is given the instant the threes unite in line.
Each chief of Legion places himself on the left of his Legion
(the guides stepping back, as before explained), dresses his
Legion to the left, commands *front*, and places himself in
front of its center.

If the third command be for the guide (on completion of
the wheel) the Grand Standard and guides advance six yards
in front of the line, and the chiefs place themselves on the
flanks of their Legions farthest from the Standard, as before
explained.

General Rules for Successive Formations.

That is, when several subdivisions arrive successively on
the line.

In all such, except formation into line by two movements,
the field officer at the head of the column or nearest the

point of rest (where right of battalion is to rest if movement be to left, or where left will rest when movement is to right) establishes his two markers (facing point of rest) on the line opposite the right and left files of the subdivisions first to arrive on the line. If formation be central, markers are placed on line in front of leading subdivision, facing each other.

In all formations from halt, markers are established at preparatory command, indicating direction in which line is to extend; if marching, they hasten toward the point of rest and are established at command MARCH. In formations on right (or left) into line, first marker is established subdivision distance to right (or left) of head of the column.

Formations front into line, they are established subdivision distance in front of head of the column.

Line is prolonged as explained in formation of battalion. When line is formed facing to rear, markers permit leading subdivisions to pass between, after which second marker closes to little less than Legion distance from the first; if formation be central, both markers close toward each other. Each guide so posts himself that his subdivision may cross line between him and guide next in front, then closes to subdivision distance.

When principles are well understood, markers may post themselves without aid of field officers, or guides act when practicable.

To Form Column of Threes on Right or Left into Line.

1. *On right* (or *left*) *into line*. 2. MARCH.

From a halt. At one, repeated by chief of the first Legion, the other chiefs of Legions order : *Forward.*

At MARCH, repeated by all the chiefs of Legions, the leading Legion executes *on right into line;* the leading three arriving at three yards from line, the chief halts the Legion and dresses it to right against markers. The other chiefs successively command: 1. *On right into line,* adding MARCH when opposite the right of their places in line, halt their Legions and dress them, as just explained.

If marching, the command to put the Legions in motion is omitted.

To Form Column of Threes, Front into Line.

1. *Right* (or *left*) *front into line.* 2. MARCH.

From a halt. At one, chief of first Legion: *Right front into line.* 2. *Double time;* chief of second Legion: 1. *Forward.* 2. *Column right;* chiefs of other Legions: 1. *Forward.* 2. *Column half right.* At MARCH, repeated, first Legion executes *right front into line* in double time; is halted at three yards from line and dressed against markers. Chief of second Legion conducts it opposite the left of its place in line, changes direction to the left, and chief commands: 1. *Right front into line.* 2. *Double time,* adding 3. MARCH when at Legion distance from line; places himself in front of its center, and when three yards from the line, halts the Legion and dresses it to the left. The other chiefs conduct their Legions to a point twice Legion distance in rear of the left of their places in line, change direction half left, and when at Legion distance from the line, conform to what has been explained for the second Legion.

If marching, omit the command *forward.*

To Form Front into Line, Faced to Rear.

1. *Right* (or *left*) *front into line, faced to rear.* 2. MARCH.

156   SCHOOL OF THE BATTALION.

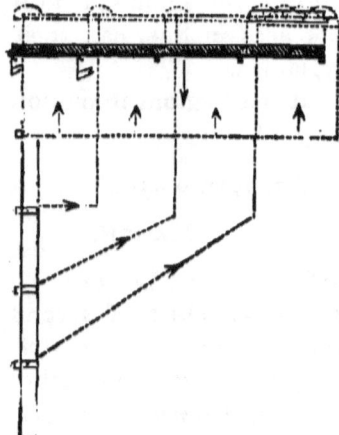

Executed as before explained, except Legions are not halted till three yards beyond the line; all the threes having arrived in line, where the Legions execute *threes left about*, halt and dress to the right.

In forming line, faced to rear, threes wheel about towards the *point of rest*.

Formation of Column of Threes into Line by two Movements.

A part of the column having changed direction to the right.

1. *Threes left.* 2. *Rear Legions left front into line.*
3. MARCH.

Chiefs, whose Legions have changed direction, repeat one and three, halt their Legions as threes unite in line, then dress to right, remaining on line till *Guides* POST.

MARCH is given as head of a Legion is about to change direction. Rear Legions execute *left front into line*.

To form line faced to rear. Column having changed direction as before, 1. *Threes right.* 2. *Rear Legions left front into line faced to rear.* 3. MARCH.

This and like formations to the left are executed similar to those explained.

To Form Column of Sections from Line.

By usual commands and means, or:

1. *Center forward.* 2. *Threes left and right.* 3. MARCH.
4. *Guide right* (or *left*).

At two, chief of right center Legion orders:

1. *Left forward.* 2. *Threes left.* Chief of left center Legion orders: 1. *Right forward.* 2. *Threes right.* Other

SCHOOL OF THE BATTALION.

chiefs: *Threes left or right*, according as they are in the right or left wing.

At MARCH, repeated, column of sections is formed. The Grand Commander marches at twelve yards from center of column. The field officers of each wing six yards from flank of the column, abreast of the leading guide; general guides abreast of the guides in rear of the column.

(The Battalion Standard Guard may lead this movement, if present.)

To Form Line from Column of Sections.

1. *Right and left front into line.* 2. MARCH.

Executed by each wing, as before explained. The markers are established for the Battalion Standard Guard [or right center Legion, if there be no Battalion Standard Guard.]

To Form Line to the Right or Left from Column of Sections.

1. *Threes right* (or *left*). 2. *Left Legions on right* (or *left*) *into line.* 3. MARCH.

The chiefs of right Legions repeat the first and third commands, halt their Legions as they unite in line, dress them to the left and remain on the left until the command *guides, posts*. The Battalion Standard Guard and Legions of the left wing execute *on right into line*. The field officer of the left wing assures the position of guide of the left Legion.

To form Column of Legions from Line.

1. *Legions right* (or *left*) *wheel.* 2. MARCH.

At one, the chiefs of Legions repeat *right wheel*. At *march* each Legion wheels as before explained, each chief halting and dressing his Legion to the left.

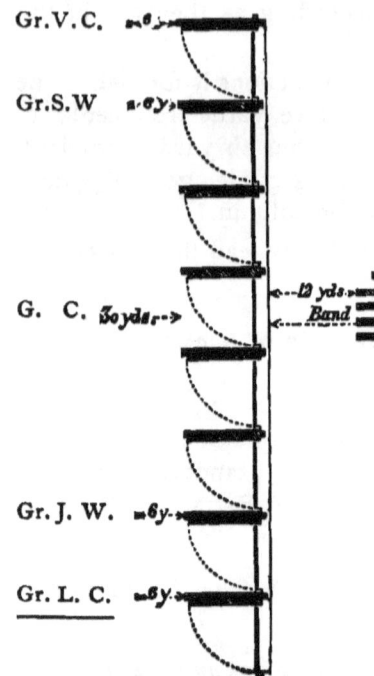

The chiefs having commanded *front*, the guides, although some of them may not be in the direction of the preceding guides, stand fast, in order that the error may not be extended through the column; the guides not in direction come into it in march.

The band is on the flank, as shown in the cut, in the drill; or may march at the head of the column if so directed.

If the battalion be in march, at the first command, the chiefs of Legions place themselves before the centers thereof; at *march* pivots halt and then turn gradually in their places; the wheel is completed as from a halt.

In column, the field officers and guides take their places, as shown in the plate, and change to the designated flank when the guide is changed. [So band changes, if not at head of column].

To Form Column and Move Forward without Halting.

1. *Continue the march.* 2. *Legions right* (or *left*) *wheel.* 3. MARCH. 4. *Forward.* 5. MARCH. 6. *Guide* (*right* or *left*).

Wheel as before; chiefs remain in front of centers. At fifth command march forward, or in the direction the field officer, at head of column, indicates for leading guide, and others follow in his trace, preserving distances.

The battalion breaks into column of squadrons, etc., in the same manner, substituting *squadrons* for **Legions**. The chief of squadron performs the same duties as chief of Legion, the junior chief places himself in the interval between the two Legions, if not already there. The guide on the right or left of the squadron is its guide.

In wheel by squadron, if there be an odd Legion, its chief commands: 1. *Forward.* 2. *Guide right* (or *left*), according as the wheel is to the right, or left, repeats the command *march*, adding: 1. *Right* (or *left*) *wheel* in time to add 2. MARCH when the Legion has advanced Legion distance, when it wheels on a fixed pivot, is halted and dressed as before explained.

To Form Column of Legions to the Rear from Line.

1. *Right of Legions, rear into column.* 2. *Threes right.* 3. MARCH.

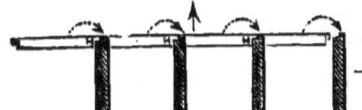

Being at a halt. At the first command each chief places himself four feet in front of the right file of his Legion facing to the right; at *threes right*, cautions the right three to wheel to the right about. The movement is executed as in divisions, q. v.

Squadrons are formed in column to the rear by similar commands and means.

To Break From the Right or Left, to March to the Left or Right from Line.

1. *Legions break from the right* (or *left*) *to march to the left* (or *right*). 2. MARCH.

Being at a halt.

At one, the chief of the first Legion orders, 1. *Forward.* 2. *Guide left.* At *march*, repeated by its chief, the right Legion moves forward, the chief commanding, 1. *Left turn*, adding 2. MARCH when the guide has advanced Legion distance; the left guide then marches on a line parallel with the front of the battalion. The second Legion executes the

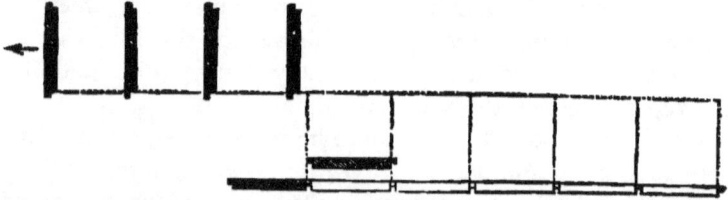

movement by the same commands and means; its chief putting it in march when the first Legion arrives opposite its left; the guide, after turning, follows in trace of the left guide of the first. The others successively execute the same movement. Don't lose distance.

To March Column Forward, Halt it, Face it to the Rear, Etc.

Executed by commands and means similar to like movements of a Legion.

To Change Direction in Column.

1. *Column right* (or *left*). 2. MARCH.

Being in march. At the first command, a marker places himself abreast of the guide, on the left of the leading subdivision. The chief of this subdivision commands: *Right wheel*, repeats the MARCH, and on completion of the wheel, commands:

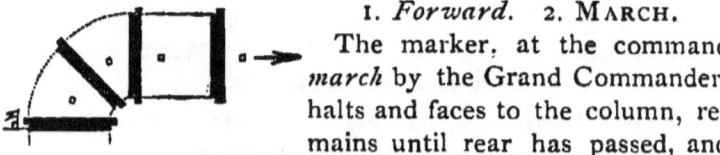

1. *Forward.* 2. MARCH.

The marker, at the command *march* by the Grand Commander, halts and faces to the column, remains until rear has passed, and returns to his place in rear of first subdivision. Other subdivisions change direction on the same ground by the same command and means.

To put column in march and change direction at the same time: 1. *Forward.* 3. *Guide left* (or *right*). 3. *Column right* (or *left*). Or, 3. *Column half right*, etc.

SCHOOL OF THE BATTALION.   161

To Form Line to the Left or Right from Column.

1. *Left* (or *right*) *into line wheel.*   2. MARCH.   3. *Guides.*
4. POSTS.

Being at a halt. At the first command chiefs of Legions caution. *left wheel;* the right guide of the leading Legion places himself facing the leading guide of the column at nearly Legion distance in front of him, so as to be opposite one of the right files of the Legion when the wheel is completed; the guide is assured in his position by the field officer at the head of the column.

At *march*, the Legions wheel to the left on fixed pivots. Each chief of Legion faces his command to observe the wheel; moves toward the point where its marching flank is to rest, and when it is near the line commands: 1. *Legion.* 2. HALT. At *halt* the chief of Legion places himself on the line, by the side of the left file of the Legion next on the right, then commands, 1. *Right.* 2. DRESS. 3. FRONT. At *dress* the Legion dresses up between its chief and its left file; the file of the right Legion, who finds himself opposite its right guide, rests his breast lightly against the left arm of their guide.

If marching, line is similarly formed, guides halt, and wheel is on fixed pivot.

To Correct Alignment.

Being at a halt. The Grand Commander, placing himself in front of the leading guide, and facing him, establishes himself and guide next in rear, then commands.

1. *Right* (or *left*) *guides.*   2. COVER.

Right guides exactly cover those in front at subdivision distance; field officers in front and rear of column facing guides assist.

1. *Right* (or *left*).   2. DRESS.

Chiefs repeat, align their subdivisions, and command, FRONT. If a Legion is out of place, chiefs give necessary preparatory (*forward, backward* or *side step*) adding *march*, at command *dress* by Grand Commander. When it approaches guide, chief halts and dresses it up to the guide.

To Form Line and Move Forward.

1. *Continue the march.* 2. *Left* (or *right*) *into line wheel.* 3. MARCH. 4. *Forward.* 5. MARCH. 6. *Guide center.*

Wheel on fixed pivots, which mark time as explained; guide remains on flank of leading Legion. At the sixth command standard and general guides step six yards to front of line, and chief of Legion places himself in front rank, as before explained.

Column of Squadrons is formed in line similarly; the chiefs of squadrons command, 1. *Right.* 2. DRESS; then (to Legion on his left), 1. (such) *Legion.* 2. FRONT; the junior chief of Legion. 1. (such) *Legion.* 2. FRONT (to Legion on his left). Odd Legion moves up to Legion distance, its guide covering guide in front, if not there.

Practice these without equalizing Legions; put column in march, Legions gain trace and distance of guides by obliques at the command of chiefs. Grand Commander assists to gain distance by causing to *mark time* or take *short steps;* those not at proper distance, etc., gain it.

To Form Column on Right or Left.

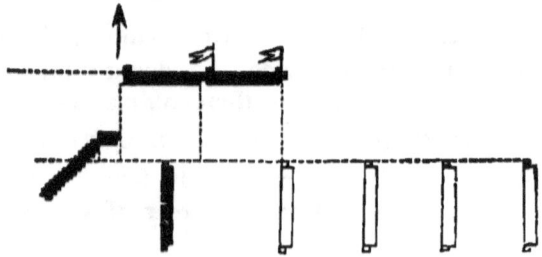

Being in march, change guide, if not there, to flank towards which movement is to be made.

1. *On right* (or *left*) *into line.* 2. MARCH.

SCHOOL OF THE BATTALION.

At one, chief of first Legion commands: *Right turn*, and repeats *march;* arriving at three yards from markers, chief halts and dresses it to the right. The other Legions continue the march, each chief giving command, 1. *Right turn*, adding, 2. MARCH, upon arriving opposite the right of its place in line, and are halted and dressed as explained for first Legion.

To Form Column Front into Line from a Halt.

1. *Right* (or *left*) *front into line.* 2. *Legions right* (or *left*) *half wheel.* 3. MARCH. 4. *Forward.* 5. MARCH. 6. *Guide left* (or *right*).

At one, chief of first Legion: 1. *Forward.* 2. *Guide left.* At second command all other chiefs of Legions caution

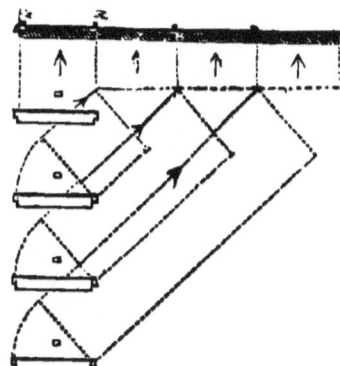

right half wheel. At third command, repeated by chiefs, the first Legion advances, and when three yards from line, is halted and dressed to left against markers; the other Legions wheel half right on fixed pivot, chiefs repeating fourth, fifth and sixth commands. At fifth command, given the instant the eighth of circle is completed, they cease to wheel and march forward. At sixth command the left guides of Legions march directly to their front.

The left of the second Legion arriving nearly opposite the right of the first, its chief commands, 1. *Left half turn*, and adds, 2. MARCH, the instant left of Legion is opposite its place in line, and its chief commands, 1.*Legion.* 2. MARCH at three yards from the line, then dresses his Legion to the left.

When left of third Legion arrives opposite right of the second, it turns half left, is halted and dressed as just prescribed, and other Legions execute successively what is prescribed for the third.

In march the movement is similarly executed, the leading Legion approaches markers with guide toward point of rest, at command of chief of Legion; if necessary, at preparatory command,

To Form Column Front into Line, Faced to Rear.

Executed as before, except Legions march three yards beyond the line; wheel about by threes, halt and are dressed toward the point of rest.

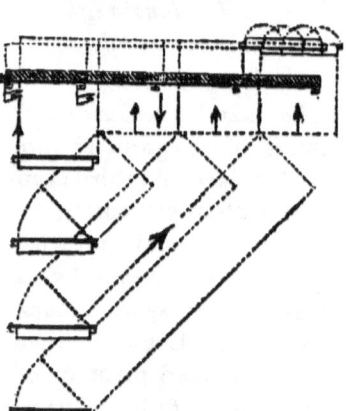

To Form Column of Legions into Line by two Movements.

The column having partly changed direction to the right,

1. *Left into line wheel.* 2. *Rear Legions left front into line.* 3. MARCH.

At one, chiefs of Legions which have changed direction caution *left wheel.* At second command, chief of each rear Legion commands, *left half wheel.* At *march* repeated by chiefs of rear Legions, those which have changed direction to right execute *left into line wheel*, rear Legions *left front into line* as before described; the chiefs of rear Legions, upon completing the half wheel, adding 1. *Forward.* 2. MARCH. 3. *Guide right.*

Column having partly changed direction to the left, line is formed by similar commands and means.

To Advance by Flank of Subdivision from Line

1. *Legions* (or *squadrons*). 2. *Right* (or *left*) forward. 3. *Threes right* (or *left*). 4. MARCH. 5. *Guide* (*right, left* or *center.*)

Each Legion (or squadron) executes *right forward*

threes right. The Grand Commander marches abreast of chiefs of leading subdivisions, twelve yards from flank, on the side of guide; or if guide be center, then on either flank, other field officers six yards outside of column abreast of subdivisions: they are covered by general guides who march abreast of rear guides.

To Form Line from Subdivisions when Marching by the Flank of Subdivisions.

1. *Legions* (or *squadrons*) 2. *Right* (or *left*) *front into line.* 3. MARCH. 4, *Battalion.* 5. HALT.

Each Legion (or squadron) executes the second command and is dressed to the right.

If executed in double time, the Grand Commander commands: *Guide center*, immediately after the command MARCH; the standard and general guides advance six yards in front of line, and chiefs of Legions place themselves on the flanks of their Legions farthest from the Battalion Standard Guard, the guides on that flank stepping back, as before explained, except the guides on the flank Legions of the battalion.

To Form Column of Subdivisions when Marching by the Flank of Subdivisions (and the reverse).

1. *Threes right* (or *left*). 2. MARCH. 3. *Guide right* (or *left*), etc.

To March by the flank of Subdivisions from Column of Threes, etc.

1. *Legions* (or *squadrons*, etc.) 2. *Column right* (or *left*). 3. MARCH. 4. *Guide right,* (*left* or *center.*)

The same command, omitting the fourth, re-forms column of threes; each chief of Legion goes to the head of his Legion; the squadrons unite in column of threes.

To Form Column of Threes from Column of Legions or Squadrons and to Form Again in Column.

1. *Legions* (or *squadrons*). 2. *Right* (or *left*) *forward.* 2. *Threes right* (or *left*). 4. MARCH.

To form again in column:

1. *Legions* (or *squadrons*). 2. *Right* (or *left*) *front into line.* 3. MARCH. 4. *Battalion.* 5. HALT.

Or 4. *Guide left* (or *right*).

The subdivisions execute these movements simultaneously. Or these movements may be executed by Legions successively, if so ordered, by designating them. They may also be executed in like manner by any subdivision of battalion.

To Close Column to Half Distance.

Being at a halt.

1. *Close column to half distance.* 2. *Forward.* 3. MARCH. 4. *Guide left* (or *right*).

At two, the chief of the leading sqadron (or Legion) commands, 1. *First squadron* (or *legion*). 2. STAND FAST; the other squadrons march forward and are successively halted and dressed to the left by their chiefs when they arrive Legion (or division) distance.

To Deploy Column.

See Legion and Display Drill.

To Form Line to the Right or Left from Column of Squadrons, etc., at Half Distance.

1. *Right* (or *left*) *into line wheel.* 2. *Left* (or *right*) *Legion on right* (or *left*) *into line.* 3. MARCH.

At one, the chiefs of right Legions caution, 1. (Such) *Legions.* 2. *Right wheel;* the left guide of the leading right Legion places himself on the line of the right guides, facing them, and so as to be opposite one of the three files on the left of his Legion; chiefs of left Legions: 1. *Forward.* 2. *Guide right.* At *march*, repeated by chiefs, the right Legions wheel into line to the right; the left Legions move forward, and when the leading one is opposite

SCHOOL OF THE BATTALION

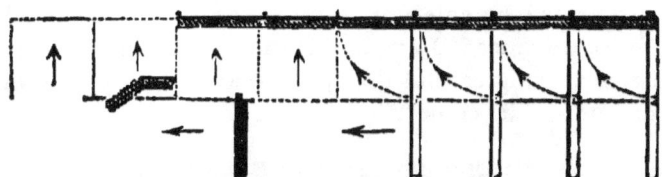

its place, executes *on right into line*. The field officer of the left wing assures the position of the guides of the left Legions.

If marching, the Grand Commander orders guide on flank towards which movement is to be made, if not there, and chiefs of Legions omit the *forward, march*.

To Form Column of Legions from Column of Squadrons, and the Reverse.

1. *Right* (or *left*), *by Legions*. 2. MARCH. 3. *Guide left* (or *right*)

Being at a halt. At the first command chiefs of right Legions: *Forward;* chiefs of left Legions: *Right oblique.* At *march*, repeated by chiefs, right Legions move forward, chiefs repeating command for guide; the chiefs of left Legions command MARCH the instant their Legions are disengaged, at which they oblique to right, shortening the step slightly. When they are in rear of right Legions their chiefs command, 1. *Forward* 2. MARCH. 3. *Guide left;* the second command is given the instant the left guide arrives in trace of the left guides of the right Legion.

1. *Form squadrons left* (or *right*) *oblique*. 2. MARCH.
3. *Battalion*. 4. HALT.

Being in column of Legions.

At one, chief of right Legion of each squadron: 1. *Forward*. 2. *Guide left;* chief of left Legion: *Left oblique*. At *march*, repeated by the chiefs, leading Legions move forward; rear Legions oblique to left. The fourth command repeated by chiefs of leading Legions, is given when they have advanced Legion distance; each chief dresses his Legion, being careful that guides cover, and places himself in front of its center.

To Change Front of Battalion.

1. *Change front on first* (or *eighth*) *Legion.* 2. *Legions right* (or *left*) *half wheel.* 3. MARCH. 4. *Forward.* 5. MARCH. 6. *Guide right* (or *left*).

At one, chiefs, if not there, place themselves in front of centers of their Legions.

At two, chief of right Legion: *Right wheel;* other chiefs caution *right half wheel.* At *march* repeated by chiefs, right Legion right wheels on fixed pivot, and its chief commands, 1. *Forward.* 2. MARCH. 3. *Guide right,* and having arrived at three yards from the line, its chief halts it and dresses it to right, against the markers.

The other Legions make half wheels to right on fixed pivots, and movement is completed similar to left front into line from column of Legions. The chiefs of rear Legions command, 1. *Right half turn,* adding. 2. MARCH, when their right guides are opposite their places in line.

(See cut.)

Oblique change of front on first (or *eighth*) *Legion* is similarly executed.

Change of front on right or left Legion and face to rear is executed, by adding *faced to rear* to the first command, and similar to front into line faced to rear from column of Legions.

Honors to be Paid by Select Knights.

ALL the honors due to official position should be paid in such manner as to reflect credit on the order.

1. The *Supreme Commander* is saluted by all standards and banners drooping, officers and Select Knights *saluting* ("officers present"), bands and trumpets sounding "Hail to the Chief."

2. *Grand Commander*, within his own jurisdiction, by all standards and banners drooping, officers saluting, Knights in ranks *present*, and trumpets sound a march.

3. *Supreme Vice-Commander* and *Supreme Lieut.-Commander;* same as Grand Commander, except trumpets give three flourishes.

4. *Grand Vice and Lieut.-Commanders* within their State, same as Grand Commander, except trumpets give two flourishes.

5. *Select Commanders* by their own Legions; same as Grand Commander, except trumpets give a flourish.

6. *Other Grand Officers* and distinguished visitors; standards and banners drooping, officers *salute* and Select Knights in ranks *present*.

7. President of the United States, or Governor within his own State; same as Select Commander.

SENTINELS face in the direction of their beat, towards the personage, and *present* when officers above the rank of Senior Workman, or Legions, cross it.

RESERVE GUARDS turn out and *present* on the approach of the Officer of the Day, Commander of the Camp, Grand Commander in his jurisdiction, and the Supreme Commander, during the day time; or at night, if so ordered.

VISITATIONS AND COURTESIES WITHOUT ARMS.

At Grand Legions, among the memorable events are the visits between Legions. If the little courtesies are gracefully attended to, they add to the dignity and pleasure of the occasion, and *per contra*, the failure to observe them detracts to that extent from the enjoyment.

When a Legion contemplates a visit to another, the Vice-Commander* calls at the quarters of the Legion to be visited, presents his Legion card and ascertains at what hour it will be convenient for that Legion to receive a visit from the Legion he represents. This being settled, the Legion forms, dressed in the uniform coat, pants, caps and belts (without swords or cuffs, unless it is a dress occasion), and appears in front of the quarters of the Legion to be visited, at the time agreed upon. Both Legions being in line, the *hand salute* is exchanged, and the visiting Legion is conducted into quarters, and is shown such attention as the Legion visited is prepared to give.

The call should be terminated before the interest fags; and, on leaving, courtesies are exchanged as before.

If a Legion is "receiving," a formal introduction by Legions may be made, and the visit shortened, that an unwieldy and crowded company may not detract from the pleasures, and give place to others.

Those who are expected to respond to sentiments, should be notified in time to collect their thoughts in a very short, pithy speech.

---

*Or Knight detailed for the duty, who should be in full dress.

Escorts of Honor.

KNIGHTS who are well drilled, and none others, should form a part of such an escort: *first*, for the credit of the Legion; *second*, that it may be considered a compliment to be so detailed and stimulated to increase attention to the tactics. The escort forms in line, the center opposite the place where the person to be escorted will present himself, with an interval between the wings to receive him and his staff, the band on the flank of the escort towards which it will march. On the appearance of the party to be escorted, he should be received with the honors due him. When he takes his place between the wings, the escort is wheeled into column of divisions, sections, or threes, and takes up the march. On leaving, the escort line is formed, and the same honors are paid as before. When the position of the escort is at a considerable distance from the point where the person is to be received, as, for instance, when a court-yard or wharf intervenes, a double line of sentinels is posted from that point to the escort, facing inward; the sentinels successively *present swords* as he passes; when he has passed six yards, they break by files into double column and re-join the escort. An officer or some Select Knight should be appointed to attend the person to be escorted, to bear any communication he may have to make to the Commander of the escort.

Escort of Legion too Large for a Small Detachment to Observe the Form Just Given.

The escort is formed in line parallel with the line of march, the right resting farthest from the point of reception. The

Commander and a Select Knight attend upon the visiting Legion. When all is ready, the Vice-Commander is given proper notice, and the Commander or Select Knight conducts the Legion to be escorted in front of and past the escort, which presents swords. The Legion to be escorted marches past in column of threes, sections, or divisions, officers and standards saluting, Knights at a carry, and halts when the rear is about fifteen yards from the band of the escort, wheels into line, and the escort marches past with the same honors exchanged as before; the Commander and Select Knight rejoining his Legion as it passes. The march is taken up by the escorted Legion, which follows the escort in column of divisions, sections or threes, halts in front of the quarters of the escorted, forms line, presents swords, and the guests march past into their quarters.

Reception and Escort of a Grand Officer.

JUSTICE and courtesy to a Grand Officer, making an official visit, requires that he should be received with all the formalities to which his rank entitles him.

The escort is commanded by the next in rank to the presidng officer; or if the body is not in session, by the chief himself.

At the command *present swords*, the honors are given as described, and the escort is conducted as before explained, according to circumstances.

For the Supreme Commander: Past Grand Officers, or Past Commanders should be selected as the escort, if practicable. For the Grand Commander: Past Select Commanders should compose the escort, if it can be conveniently done, unless they should happen to be awkward in ranks, in which case they ought not to be selected in any event, if well drilled Select Knights can supply their places.

Dress Parade.

THE Field Officers are dismounted. From the nature of his duties, it is most appropriate for the Grand Recorder to act as Adjutant, but, it having been made the duty of the Grand Marshal, he, or some *well qualified* Knight should perform this especial duty.

The battalion is formed as before explained, [or if it be of but one Legion, its divisions are officered and are treated as Legions, the Select Commander acting as Grand Commander, and the Recorder as Adjutant.]

The Grand Commander, as commanding officer, takes his post at a convenient distance in front of the center, facing the line (generally a distance equal to about one-half its front) and stands with arms folded until just before the command to *present*, when he comes to *attention*.

The Grand Commander's staff may form in line six yards in his rear.

The Acting Adjutant having commanded *guides*, *posts*, directs the first Commander to bring his Legion to *parade rest*. Each Commander in succession, commencing on the right, faces about, and commands:

1. (Such) *Legion*. 2. *Carry*. 3. Swords. 4. *Parade*. 5. Rest, and faces to the front.

The Acting Adjutant then commands, Sound off, and takes the position of *parade rest*. The band, commencing to play in common time, marches six yards to the front, then to the left past the left of the line, and back over the same ground to its place, playing in quick time, giving a flourish before starting, after the counter-march at the left, and on its return to the right.

The Acting Adjutant steps two yards to the front, faces to the left, and commands:

1. *Battalion.* 2. ATTENTION. 3. *Carry.* 4. SWORDS.
5. *Rear open order.*

Aligns the guides of the rear rank, again comes to the front and commands, 6. MARCH, verifies the alignments, commands, 7. FRONT, and passes in rear of the line of commanders to the center, turns to the right, marches to a point midway between the Grand Commander and the line occupied by the commanders, faces about, and commands:

1. *Present.* 2. SWORDS.

To this the Grand Commander raises his chapeau in acknowledgment. The Acting Adjutant then faces about, salutes the Grand Commander and says:

Sir, the parade is formed.

The Grand Commander, saluting with the hand:

Take your post, Sir Knight.

The Acting Adjutant passes by the right of the Grand Commander, two yards to his rear, faces to the right, marches one yard to the left of the Grand Commander and two yards retired and faces the battalion. The Grand Commander now draws his sword, commands, *Carry,* SWORDS, and exercises the battalion in the manual, concluding with, *Order,* SWORDS. He directs the Acting Adjutant to *Receive the reports,* and returns his sword.

The Acting Adjutant retraces his steps to the point at which he saluted the Grand Commander, and commands:

1. **Recorders to front and center.* 2. MARCH.

At the first command, the Recorders come to a *carry;* at the second, they step one yard to the front and face to the center; the drum-major also steps one yard forward, and faces to the left. At *march,* they close on the center in front of and between the standard and Acting Adjutant, one yard

---

* *Vice-Commanders* or *right files* may be substituted for *Recorders* if desired.

from the former, and successively face to the front. The Acting Adjutant then commands, REPORT. At this command the drum-major* and Recorders, commencing on the right, successively salute and report, *Band present or accounted for*, or (so many) *absent*. The Recorders report (such) *Legion No. — present or accounted for*, or give the number present and the number absent. When completed, the Acting Adjutant commands :

1. *Recorders.* 2. *Outward.* 3. FACE. 4. *To your posts.* 5. MARCH.

Then they all retrace their steps and resume *order arms.*

The Acting Adjutant faces about, salutes, and says, *Sir, all present, or accounted for;* or he reports the number absent.

The Grand Commander acknowledges the salute and says, *Publish the orders, Sir Knight.* The Acting Adjutant, facing the battalion, says:

Attention to orders,

Returns his sword and reads the orders. After which he draws his sword, faces about, salutes the Grand Commander and reports :

Sir, the orders are published.

The Grand Commander acknowledges the salute, and directs the Adjutant to

Dismiss the Parade, Sir Knight.

At which the Acting Adjutant, facing the Battalion, commands:

Parade is Dismissed.

The Commanders, Vice-Commanders, and Lieut.-Commanders now return their swords, face to the center, step off

---

*The drum-major before making his report, salutes by bringing his staff to a vertical position, the head of the staff up and opposite the left shoulder.

at the same time with the Acting Adjutant, close upon the center, and successively face to the front, the Field Officers on the flanks. The two nearest the center preserve an interval for the Acting Adjutant, who passes through, one yard to the rear, halts, faces about, steps into his place, and commands:

   1. *Forward.* 2. *Guide center.* 3. MARCH.

The band plays, and when within five yards of the Grand Commander, the Acting Adjutant commands:

   1. *Officers.* 2. HALT.

At the second command the officers halt and salute with the hand; the music ceases; the hands remain at the visor till the salute is acknowledged, and drop at the same time with the Grand Commander's hand, who gives such instruction as he desires, which concludes the ceremony, and the officers disperse; the band plays; the Senior Workmen command:

   1. (Such) *Legion.* 2. *Carry.* 3. SWORDS. 4. *Close Order.* 5. MARCH.

At the command *march*, the Senior Workmen march the Legions to their quarters and dismiss them, as they may have previously have been instructed.

It would add much to the display if, after the parade is dismissed, the Legions should march off in echelon, Legion front, beginning on the right; the second Legion starting when the first has marched Legion distance, or half Legion distance.

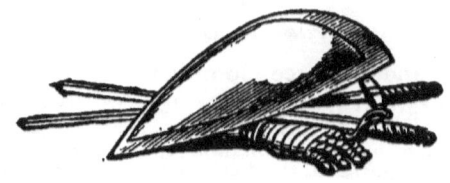

Review.

Reviewing officer takes post in front of the center of battalion, the point being indicated by a marker, or standard, previously established. The Acting Adjutant also posts markers at points where the column will have to change direction in order that the right flank, in passing, shall be at six or eight yards from the reviewing officer, whose staff, or other grand officers, are in his rear.

The officer in command, being in front of and facing the center, commands:

1. *Prepare for review.* 2. *Rear open order.* 3. March. 4. Front.

At the command *march*, the ranks are opened and the lines are dressed as before explained.

Officer in command, seeing the ranks aligned, returns to the right of the line of chiefs of Legions, faces to the left, commands Front, and passing to the front of this line of officers, places himself six yards in front of the line of field officers, opposite the center and facing to the front. The reviewing officer now approaches a few yards and halts, when the officer in command faces about and commands:

1. *Present.* 2. Swords.

The officers, standards, and Knights *present*, and if the reviewing officer be the grand officer, the band plays a march or trumpets flourish, according to his rank. Officer in command faces about and salutes with the sword. The reviewing officer acknowledges the salute by raising his chapeau, the band ceases to play, and the officer in command again faces the line and commands:

REVIEW.

1. *Carry.* 2. SWORDS.

He joins the reviewing officer, who proceeds to the right of the band, and passing to the left in front of the line of chiefs of Legions, returns in rear of the rear rank, the band playing until he leaves the right to return to his station.

The officer in command now returns to his post in front of the center and commands:

1. *Close order.* 2. MARCH.

Which having been executed, he adds:

1. *Legions (divisions or sections), right wheel.*
2. MARCH.

At the second command, the Legions break into column of Legions (divisions or sections).

The band wheels and marches so that its rear rank will be nine yards in advance of the leading chief of Legion. The Grand Vice Commander, Grand Lieut.-Commander and Grand Workman on the left of the column.

The officer in command now commands:

1. *Pass in review.* 2. *Forward.* 3. *Guide right.* 4. MARCH.

The band plays; the column advances and changes direction to the left, and again to the left, at points indicated, so as to pass about six yards in front of the reviewing officer, and without command from the officer in command, who takes his place three yards in advance of the chief of the leading Legion (or officer in command of the leading subdivision), after the second change of direction. The band, having passed the reviewing officer, wheels to the left out of column, takes post in front and facing him, where it remains till the rear of the column has passed, when it countermarches to the rear and returns to its place before the review, ceasing to play when the column approaches its original position. If there is more than one Legion (not in battalion formation) each band ceases to play when the rear of its Legion has passed the reviewing officer, and follows in its rear until its Legion is halted, when it passes by the rear to its place on the right.

When the column is passing in review, the officers and standards *salute*, each commencing six yards from the reviewing officer, and resuming the carry when six yards past; the Knights in line retain the *carry*.

If the reviewing officer be entitled to it, the trumpets flourish, etc., as before explained, and the band continues to play.

The drum-major, marching in review, passes the staff between the right arm and the body, the head to the front, and salutes with the left hand.

In saluting, all the officers turn the head and look toward the reviewing officer, who acknowledges only the salutes of the officer in command and the standards.

The officer in command having saluted, places himself, if mounted, on the right of the reviewing officer, and there remains until his battalion has passed, when he rejoins the battalion. The head of the column having executed a second change of direction to the left, after passing the reviewing officer, the officer in command commands *guide left*, and when it arrives on its original ground, wheels it into line, ranks are opened and swords are presented as before; this being acknowledged, terminates the review.

General Parade.

GENERAL PARADES are unfortunately often marred by some one, who seems to have little regard for well devised plans; among Select Knights, however, a cheerful obedience to law is expected from all.

It requires very little individual effort to conform to rules, and their general observance would add materially to the pleasure at general gatherings.

When Grand Legions are to form for street parade, the observance of the following rules is important.

1. GENERAL HEADQUARTERS should be established; its chief and staff prepared at all hours to furnish information concerning existing orders; localities of grand or subordinate Legions; assignment of quarters for new arrivals; a post office for mailing or distributing letters to individuals (or Legions), etc., rosters, alphabetically or systematically arranged, so as to be of some use. In short, a place where any reasonable demand would be met with courteous and intelligent response.

2. GRAND LEGIONS should have headquarters, with some one constantly in attendance who could give information concerning the subordinate legions or Select Knights of that command.

3. HEADQUARTERS for every subordinate Legion present, and at least an intelligent servant left in charge, who could receive and properly deliver messages, letters, or orders left in the absence of the Select Knights.

4. TO INSURE ALL THIS, commanding officers should be ordered to report their arrivals at Grand Legion headquarters and leave a duplicate list of the Select Knights with their command, as well as the ladies and band accompanying it; at their own headquarters to keep a register of the locality of the private quarters of each individual. At stated hours every Knight should report at his Legion headquarters, in order that all may feel some confidence in expecting to find their friends there at that time; or general or special information concerning the parade, which should be given at roll-call.

Grand Commanders should report at general headquarters immediately on their arrival.

Orders should be promptly sent to Grand Commanders, who should require a staff officer to promptly deliver them to subordinate commanders. At the risk of appearing harsh it is asserted and emphasized, that disobedience of lawful orders ought to be followed with prompt and effectual discipline. Delay blunts the point of discipline.

Nothing wearies men in ranks so much as unnecessary waiting and frequent vexatious halts. This is demoralizing to an army, therefore *promptness is the great essential.* Let it be understood *and felt* that the column, announced to move at a given hour, will receive the command to forward march at the time specified, and not a moment later.

At the time fixed for forming battalions the trumpet sounds and the Legions march to the battalion parade grounds.

If Legions are to move independently, still the oldest Legion is on the right, formed as prescribed; fifteen yards from its left is the right of the band of the next in rank, and so on.

Grand Officers in command, and their staffs, should be mounted or go on foot. To ride in carriages is not military, nor is it exactly "the thing" for a chief in command. He takes position in front of the center of the line or on the flank of the column in drill, etc., but in a street parade should ride at the head of the Grand Legion, so that the rear of his escort will be fifteen yards from the band of his leading Legion.. The Grand Vice-Commander rides at his left a little retired; the staff is in their rear, in column of sections, etc. The Grand Standard Bearer should carry a banner, with the arms or name of the State thereon, if the Grand Standard is not borne by him.

The instant his line is formed, the Grand Commander should send a staff officer to the Supreme Commander, or the commander in chief, to inform him of the fact.

A bugler should accompany each Grand Commander to sound the *attention, forward, halt*, etc., that all the Legions may move together. The commander in chief should also be accompanied by a bugler, and his signals be promptly repeated by each Grand Commander's bugler.

Bands near together should never play at the same time, and catch the step from the last drum beat, *not* from the step it happens to have. Bands should also be instructed to take the full step and maintain their proper distances.

The distance between Grand Divisions (Grand Legions) should be twenty yards.

A Grand Legion, too small to form a Grand Division, should join with others and form, according to seniority, as one Grand Division.

A maneuver that would retard the rear of the column ought not to be permitted. If the leading Legion, by permission, executes any movement that causes it to lose ground, it should immediately take the double step to regain its distance. Each Legion either shortens or lengthens its steps, or executes some movement that will enable it to retain its proper place in the column; or Legions execute maneuvers successively from the right of Grand Divisions. A signal from the commander in chief, repeated by Grand Commanders, would enable maneuvers to be commenced simultaneously on the right of each Grand Division, and followed in succession by Legions, or simultaneously by every Legion in the column, according to previously promulgated orders.

GENERAL PARADE.

Gaps in the column, or the crowding together of grand or subdivisions should never be permitted, and each commanding officer ought to caution his subordinates and the guides on these points; complimenting them if they do well, and severely censuring any violation of this rule. The carelessness of a single officer or Knight will destroy more of the harmony and beauty of the display than a whole Grand Division can neutralize; if, indeed, it can be overcome at all.

To Pass in Review at General Parade.

If the column is to pass in review before the Supreme Commander, the Grand Commanders, successively from the right, when they approach the station of the Supreme Commander command:

1. *Pass in review.* 2. *Guide right*

And the column continues the march, the bands do not wheel out of column, but if near together are careful to cease playing in time for the one in the rear to commence at fifteen yards from the station of the Supreme Commander.

When a column passes in review it ought to be by Legion or divison front, certainly not less than section front.

Sword Signals.

The commands at a funeral are often grating to the feelings, seem cold and harsh; hence, signals should be used when practicable. They should be well learned before attempted in public. Take the position of first motion of attention before giving and resume it after each signal.

Attention. Step four yards to left of leading guide, if Legion be in column, or in front when in line, that Knights may plainly see. 1. Reverse the sword, grasp blade near the point with right hand, hilt up. 2. Swing it by a wrist movement in a circle close to right side, and pause when hilt is up, blade perpendicular, hand at hight of shoulder.

Attention. *When about the grave or coffin*: 1. Drop sword blade by the left, close in front of body, to position of *parade rest*, the right hand resting on the helmet. 2 Raise sword by its helmet in front of center of the body, hand as high as chin. 3. Lower sword to the ground, resuming first motion.

Halt. Sword being vertical, hilt up. 1. Raise the right hand and drop the sword to left over the head, catch gripe in left hand, both arms extended, sword horizontal. 3. (For execution) bring sword far enough to front to pass the chapeau, lower it with both hands horizontally to the height of hips.

March. 1. Bring sword hilt to the front, so that the blade shall be inclined upward forty-five degrees. 2. By a decided motion extend the right arm to its full length in direction of the sword.

From right take distance. 1. Slip right hand to center of the blade, instantly raise the hand, arm extended, point of sword in direction column is moving, blade horizontal. 2. Reseize blade near the point and give signal for March.

From center deploy. 1. Seize blade by middle as before, raise it quickly, point to right, gripe over the head, arm extended, blade horizontal. 2. Give the signal to *march.*

Close intervals same as *from center deploy.*

To close to wheeling distance, being at open order. Same as *from right take distance.*

Cross. SWORDS. The *attention,* as explained for position about the coffin; then, 1. Seize blade with left hand near the guards, drop right hand to the side. 2. Raise sword perpendicularly, the gripe in front of the face. 3. As a signal for execution, lower sword until the left hand is at the belt buckle.

Carry. SWORDS. The second and third motions of *cross swords.*

1. *Present.* 2. SWORDS. 1. Re-seize the gripe and come to a *present.* 2. Drop the sword point and hand to position of a *salute,* which is the signal of execution.

Carry. SWORDS. 1. Bring the sword from *officers present* to *present.* 2. Resume the *carry,* as signal of execution.

Parade. REST. Signal of *attention,* for about the coffin; then, 1. Sieze the gripe with left hand near the guards, the right grasping the helmet, back of hands to front, sword vertical in front of center of body, point down, hilt at belt buckle. 2. Raise sword with both hands as high as the chin. 3. Lower sword by quick motion to position of *parade rest.*

Reverse. SWORDS. 1. Reseize the gripe with the right hand and take position of first motion of *reverse.* 2. Execute *reverse swords.* The instant the sword is in position is the signal of execution.

Return. SWORDS. Face the Legion, give the sword a sweep in a circle down to the right, bringing it up to a *present,* and return the sword as prescribed. As the *third motion* is the signal for execution, all return their swords at the same instant.

Band to play. Face the band, extend right arm to its full length in direction of sword. 2. Withdraw the hand, *carry swords,* face to the proper front, and the band should commence to play.

Band to cease playing. Face the band and give the same signal as for *band to play.*

If it is desired to have the band commence playing when the Legion *presents swords,* the signal for present swords may answer for both, or the band is instructed to commence the instant swords are presented.

Bugle Signals.

These should be made a part of the instruction. The *assembly* is the signal for forming in ranks; if habitually sounded before forming the Legion it will be learned without effort.

The signals for drill are taught one or two at a time, until all are familiar with them.

A trumpet call embraces both the preparatory and executory commands, which are promptly repeated orally by the officers of subdivisions. Their frequent use will insure quick recognition, and the beauty of the signal drill will then be fully appreciated.

Movements to the right are on the ascending chord; corresponding movements to the left are corresponding signals on the descending chord; and changes of gait are all upon the same notes.

A person having "an ear for music" can easily learn to play upon the bugle or trumpet, and the principal signals can be learned in a surprisingly short space of time. It requires less study and practice than is necessary to commit the ritual to memory.

BUGLE SIGNALS.

1. ASSEMBLY OF MUSICIANS.

2. ASSEMBLY.

3. RECALL.

4. DRESS PARADE.

5. FLOURISH FOR REVIEW.

6. ATTENTION.

7. FORWARD.

8. HALT.

9. QUICK TIME.

BUGLE SIGNALS.

10. DOUBLE TIME

11. CHARGE.

12. GUIDE RIGHT.

13. GUIDE LEFT.

14. GUIDE CENTRE.

15. THREES RIGHT.

16. THREES LEFT.

17. THREES RIGHT ABOUT.

18. THREES LEFT ABOUT.

19. COLUMN RIGHT.

20. COLUMN LEFT.

21. RIGHT OBLIQUE.
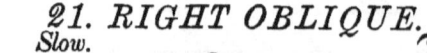

22. LEFT OBLIQUE.

23. RIGHT FRONT INTO LINE.

24. LEFT FRONT INTO LINE.

25. FACE TO THE REAR.

26. ON RIGHT INTO LINE.

27. ON LEFT INTO LINE.

28. LEGION RIGHT WHEEL.

29. LEGION LEFT WHEEL.

30. DEPLOY.

31. TO THE REAR.

32. BY THE RIGHT FLANK.

33. BY THE LEFT FLANK.

34. FUNERAL MARCH.

Very slow.

Repeat at will.

Award of Prize

AND RULES FOR COMPETITIVE DRILLS.

The "pomp and circumstance" of Select Knightly gatherings are often depreciated, nevertheless these displays form a powerful adjunct for the development of our numerical strength and influence.

On such occasions the test of skill in military maneuvers is not the least among the attractions.

In such drills there must be judges to "keep tally" and determine the relative merits of contestants.

The most skillful Board of Judges cannot, with any degree of certainty, arrive at correct conclusions unless—

1. They are familiar with the system of drill used.

2. Constantly near the Legion drilling; placing themselves on its flanks and in those proximate positions from which they can observe every movement to the best advantage.

3. They must score and record the degree of merit each separate movement is entitled to, and that before another movement is executed.

4. Each judge must have the same method of scoring and understand it before the drilling commences.

5. The Legions should, as far as practicable, *execute the same movements in the same order*, and within the same limit of time.

The judges can *guess* as to the comparative merit of different Legions, but they cannot satisfactorily "score" them except upon the foregoing basis. To undertake to make up a score after the drilling is over is out of the question.

When the aggregate score is made up, the chiefs of the several competing Legions are notified of the time and place fixed for the public announcement and awarding of the prize, that each with his command may be present.

The following is recommended as a basis for

Rules for Competitive Drills.

1. Each Legion shall consist of twenty-four* Select Knights and three† as officers, all of its own membership.‡

2. Each Legion shall drill separately, and in the order of rank,‖ for forty minutes, unless the time be changed by unanimous consent of the officers in command of competing Legions.

3. Three or five§ disinterested experts shall be selected by the Grand Commander, as a board of Judges, but they shall not be known as such to any others, until announced on the field.¶

4. The judges shall select their own method of scoring.

5. They shall have exclusive control of the field and Legion during the drill.

---

*Not less than eighteen nor more than forty-eight. Fix the number 18, 24, 36, or 48.
†One Commander or three Com. and V. & L. C. or six Com. V. & L. C. and Standard Guard.
‡It would be unjust to award a prize to a command permitted to pick or hire men from other Legions or organizations for the occasion.
‖The oldest has precedence and post of honor on every occasion; it would therefore be anything but fair to let it usurp the place belonging by right to a junior, or require the latter to hazard its right by lot.
§Five is better. ¶Selected in time to become familiar with the system of drill to be used.

RULES FOR COMPETITIVE DRILL.

6. Except the judges, the Legion drilling, its band and standard guard, no person whatever his rank or position may be, shall remain (even for a moment) on the field during or between drills.

7. Legions may drill with or without music, but the judges may require any movements to be executed without music, and the cadence shall be noted irrespective of the time kept by the band.

8. The chiefs in charge of Legions shall report at headquarters on the field thirty minutes before the contest is to commence; at which time they may determine by ballot whether the drill shall be witnessed by contestants before his Legion has drilled. If not determined, then there shall be no such restriction.

9. Legions shall cease drilling at the second sound of the *recall* (made five minutes after its first sounding), at which the next Legion shall be ready, having been informed as to the time, and at the *forward*, shall march on the field.

10. Want of promptness in responding to signals shall be treated as errors and marked against the delinquent.

11. No movement shall be executed that is not provided for in the authorized tactics.

12.* A schedule of movements shall be prepared by the judges. This may embrace any movement included in the "School of the Knight," "Manual of the Sword," excepting the silent manual, and "School of the Legion."

13. Any movement passed will be marked "o," and cannot be taken up afterwards, except by unanimous consent of chiefs before the drill, but the omitted movements only, shall be executed after the programme is completed and by distinct understanding as to what particular (*omitted*) movements will be taken up, and their order of execution.

---

*This is not difficult for well drilled Legions, but if desired can be excepted. If the contest is likely to be close, a schedule, though simple, is almost if not quite indispensable. Better let it be practiced any desired time before the drill than dispense with it.

14. The schedule shall be delivered to each chief of Legion twice the number of minutes allowed for the schedule drill, but not exceeding one hour, before his time to march on the field.

15. Ten minutes may be allowed for display movements not embraced in the schedule, but these shall not be considered in any way in making up the score.

16. Each Legion shall march on the field and halt in line, in front of the judges' quarters. The chief commands, *Present,* SWORDS, faces about, salutes and reports: *Sir,* —— *Legion No.* — *of* ————, *awaits your orders,* and hands to the judges a paper signed by him, and containing these words:

"I certify on honor, that the every man in line of —— Legion No. — of ————, now before you and reported for drill, are *bona fide* members thereof, that I received the schedule for this drill at — o'clock — M. this day, and was not before that hour apprised of any movement contained therein, nor had I any previous information of any movement that would be required in this drill.

Date, ...   Signed, ...

Presentation of Awards.

The Legions being notified, march to the designated place, and each forms as the side of a hollow square, at the point indicated by an aid, or the Drill Committee; or two Legions may form each side of the square, if room is an object. The chiefs form the front and center of their Legions, bring their commands to *parade rest,* face about, and assume the same position. The chief, when addressed by the Judges, Committee, or person selected to make the formal presentation, comes to *attention* and *salutes* and so stands during the presentation. He makes suitable response, then, facing about, commands:

1. *Legion.*   2. ATTENTION.

and returns his sword.   He then announces: "Comrades, you

have been awarded the first (or such) prize for ——————
Behold the trophy that your skill hath secured."

Whereupon the Vice-Commander orders:

   1. *Present.* 2. S<small>WORDS</small>.

and the trumpets give three flourishes.

C<small>HIEF</small>—"Receive the reward of merit, and may it never be sullied by any unworthy act of a Select Knight of our number."

The Standard Guard, or previously designated squad, under direction of its chief, carry swords, advance to within a yard or two of the trophy, and *present swords.* The Commander says: "Take this trophy, bear it in triumph to your comrades, and guard it with jealous care."

The Standard Bearer, or designated Knight carries, returns swords, and takes possession of the trophy, marches back to place, and faces to the front. The Vice-Commander commands

   1. *Carry.* 2. *Swords.*

and the officer who commanded in the drill wheels the Legion into subdivisions so that the trophy bearers and guard can occupy a prominent position in the center of the column, and the Legion marches off.

Camps and Camping.

THE forms of camps depends upon the number to be accommodated, the kind of tents, and the nature and extent of the ground; which latter should be susceptible of good drainage, and situated near good water.

The terms *flank, front, rank, file,* etc., are applied to camps the same as to Knights in column, etc.

A Legion could "pitch its tents" in the form of a cross, with the decorated quarters of its commander in the center. Or, camps may be formed as a hollow square, the tents facing toward the large area within; the commander's tent in its center, or on the side opposite and facing the opening left for ingress and egress; kitchen in rear.

IN BATTALION CAMPS the tents are arranged in column of squadrons (or Legions); the tents of the first squadron (or Legion) faced to the rear; those of the second faced to the front, forming an avenue (street) or "squadron (or Legion) parade-ground" between. Those of the third squadron (or Legion) are faced to the rear, and so on.

The principal Legion officers' tents are in line parallel to the flank of the column, facing the squadron avenues, opposite their own Legion quarters. The Select Commanders and other Legion officers are on the flank nearest to their commanders' tent.

The principal Grand Officers' tents, when practicable, are in the center of the line of the Legion officers' tents, otherwise they are in rear of its center, parallel to and facing it.

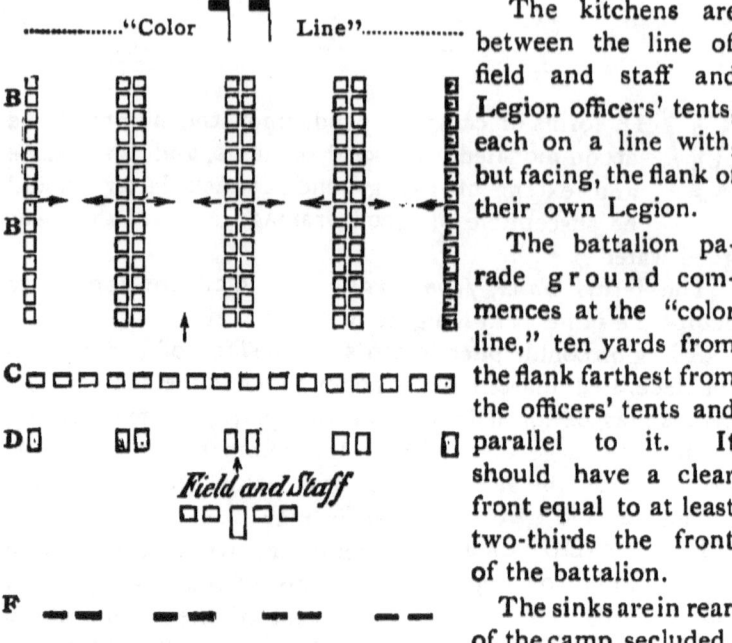

The kitchens are between the line of field and staff and Legion officers' tents, each on a line with, but facing, the flank of their own Legion.

The battalion parade ground commences at the "color line," ten yards from the flank farthest from the officers' tents and parallel to it. It should have a clear front equal to at least two-thirds the front of the battalion.

The sinks are in rear of the camp, secluded.

Camps in column of Legions are similar in form to that of the camp in column of squadrons.

The front of a camp (flank of the column) is nearly equal to that of a battalion, and the number and length of the ranks of tents and width of the avenues vary with the strength of the Legions; but there should be the same number of tents in each line, and, if necessary, Legions are temporarily consolidated. (See page 152.)

The interval between files of tents is two yards. The distance between ranks (back to back) two yards; between ranks facing each other, forming the avenues, about fifteen (never less than six) yards, depending upon the number, etc. The distance from flank of column to line of officers' tents,

---

*B B, Lines of Knights' tents with their avenues. C, Line of principal Legion officers' tents. D, Kitchens. F, Sinks.

about fifteen yards. From officers' tents to kitchens, and from kitchens to field and staff, about fifteen yards.

The avenues should be ditched (guttered) on the sides like a street in a city; and if the weather is threatening, the tents are ditched and the loose earth thrown against the canvas, to prevent overflow and dampness inside.

If cots and mattresses cannot be conveniently secured, drive forked sticks into the ground, three feet apart, more or less; place a strong stick across; about six feet distant a like arrangement; lay spring boards across, and place clean straw upon this, covering with large shawl or blanket. These boards should be secured at one end to keep them from slipping, and be left free at the other end to admit of spring when a person lies upon it. Narrow strips (from head to foot); or split small saplings, place their flat sides up, securing one end, will make a comfortable bed, which should be one and a half to two feet from the ground.

The commander should be held responsible for the cleanliness of his Legion quarters, and the officer of the day should see that this duty is not neglected.

THE "QUARTERMASTER."

The Treasurer *ex-officio*, or some Knight who is careful in the use of money (*i. e.*, not extravagant) should be detailed as Acting Quartermaster ["A. Q. M."] with such assistants as are necessary. He should have a pocket cash and blank receipt book, keeping accurate and detailed account of receipts and disbursements; and should render a full detailed report, accompanied by vouchers, at the close of the convention. This should be critically examined by a committee and reported upon, and the facts noted of record.

The object is to supervise the acts of the fiduciary officer, which ought never to be neglected; and it is also an act of justice to him that every one may feel that the affairs have been faithfully managed; or, if not, the errors may be avoided next time; besides the record, if preserved, will be a guide for future operations.

A Legion going into camp, or on an excursion, should estimate the probable cost *per capita*, and each Knight should pay his *pro rata* to the A. Q. M. with which to purchase tickets, etc. He superintends the detail for handling baggage, and makes all the necessary purchases for camps and general use. This enables the Legion to form and march promptly; prevents much of the rushing excitement of a crowd, and reduces the expenses by wholesale purchases, etc.

The A. Q. M. should be chief in his department, subject only to the orders of the commander, and his authority should be cheerfully recognized.

A "ladies' escort" is formed from those members who are unable to march with the Legion; but the A. Q. M. and assistants attend to all the baggage.

Correspondence and Orders.

Orders are general or special, and are numbered in regular series, commencing with the administration of the Grand Officer.

General orders contain whatever may be desired to be made known to the whole jurisdiction.

Special orders are such as concerns individuals or Legions that need not be published to all—such as permission to appear in public, to receive petition out of time, etc.

All orders state at their head the source, place, date and number; at its foot the name and rank of the officer giving it. If printed, copies are made *official* by the true signature of the Recorder himself, or a staff officer, thus:

HEADQUARTERS
GRAND LEGION OF NEW YORK.

—————, February 1st, 1882.

General Orders }
No. — }

* * * * * *

By command of

Sir James E. Knapp, Grand Commander.

W. F. BOHN, Grand Recorder.

Official, ————

[If the signature is printed the same, or other recognized staff officer can make it "official."]

Orders may be put in the form of letters, but the strict military form is better. If printed, they should be on uniform (note) size of paper, suitable to be bound with the proceedings or kept in files.

Written Official Communications

From a Grand or subordinate commander, to those under his command, may be by a staff officer, or Recorder. In other cases, by the officer or Knight himself. Official communications from a Legion pass through the Grand Commander to the Grand Commander of another jurisdiction, and *vice versa*, but between Legions they go direct.

Official communications, as a rule, whether from inferior to superior or *vice versa*, pass through the intermediate Commanders, *e. g.* A Select Knight wishing to send an official letter to the Supreme Commander addresses it regularly on the inside to him, but forwards it to his own commander, who indorses it and sends it to the Supreme Commander. The response comes through the same channels, addressed on the inside to the Select Knight; or the same paper is indorsed and returned through the proper channels, but may be signed by a staff officer. It is better that official letters as a rule, be written on letter paper and folded twice, (in three folds) parallel with the writing. Indorsements are made on the back, as shown below.

The top here is the back of the left side of the written page; indorsement for filing is made on the back of the fold at the top of the written page. The perpendicular lines represent the folds. The horizontal rulings are in red ink.

Louisville, Ky.,—'83.	*Hd. Qrs.* —— *Legion No.* —	*Hd. Qr. G. Supreme Legion, U. S.*
GRANT, H. B.,	————, 1883.	————, 1883.
Col. [Give Rank.]	*Courteously forwarded, with the recommendation that the request, which appears to be just and reasonable, be granted.*	*Courteously returned. The order cannot now be changed, because * * By command of*—— —————— *Gr. Rec.*
Asks for suspension of Gen. Ord. No. —, *until his Manual, now in hands of the printer, can be submitted.*		
	—————— *Com'der.*	*Hd. Qrs. Gr. Legion of* ————, 1883.
	Hd. Qrs. Gr. Legion of ————, 1883.	*Courteously returned. The attention of Sl't Kt. Grant is respectfully directed to the endorsement of the Gr. C.*
	Approved, and courteously forwarded. If the committee must select a manual, this will give wider range and prevent widespread dissatisfaction, also diminish the chances for injustice to fraters.	*By order of* —————— *Gr. Com.* —————, *Gr. Rec.* [etc., etc.]
Rec'd, Hd. Qrs.— ...., 1883.	—————, *Gr. C.*	

The whole matter can be thoroughly understood and regularly traced by the indorsements. When once understood it is simple and very convenient. It is strictly military.

Contents................ 4	Port swords...... 30
Preface........ .... 6, 7	Order swords................. 30
Indorsement.. 8	Charge........ 31
Vocabulary of military terms 9, 10	Right shoulder swords........ 31
School of Select Knight.. 11	Support (from shoulder)....... 31
Introduction.................. 11	Rear rest swords.............. 32
Commands.................... 12	Reverse....................... 32
Position...... 12	Sword arms rest............... 33
Rest: in place; parade..... 13, 14	Parade rest................... 33
Attention..................... 14	Open files.................... 34
Break ranks... 14	Cross swords .... ,.... 34
Eyes right and left............ 14	Kneel and rest on swords..... 35
Salutes with hand............ 14	Return swords................ 36
Facings: right; left; about.... 15	Secure swords 36
Steps and cadence.........16, 17	Inspection swords............ 37
Balance step.................. 17	Uncover...................... 37
To March in common time.... 17	Silent Manual................ 38
To halt....................... 17	The Salutes........ 14, 28, 29, 39
" march quick time....... 17, 18	Officer's School........... 40
" march double time...... 18, 19	Legion and Staff.............. 41
" mark time................. 18	The Band................... 42
Short step 18	School of Legion (17 plates). 44
To change step............... 18	Formations................... 46
" march backward........... 18	Double ranks................. 48
" march to rear............. 18	To dismiss Legion............ 48
" march side wise........... 19	" open ranks........... ..... 48, 49
" dress. 20	" march in line........ 49
" march forward...... 20	" halt in line 49
" march by flank............ 21	" wheel in line.............. 49
" change direction. 21	" incline and turn....... 50, 51
" put column in motion and change direction...... 21, 22	" march by flank. 51
	" march threes to front..... 52
" halt a column.............. 22	" change direction of column. 52
" form line from column..... 22	" halt column 53
" oblique................... 22	" oblique in column.......... 53
Wheelings ... ,.......... 23–25	" march column to rear 53
Double rank.................. 25	" line to right, etc., from 3's.. 54
Sword Manual (22 plates)... 26	" form line on the right, etc.. 55
Draw swords 27	Line to front 1 or 2 ranks...56, 57
Carry swords 27, 28	" face and march to rear.... 58
Present swords................ 28	To break threes to rear...... 58
Officers present or "salute"... 28	Route step.................... 59
Salute for Standard...... 28, 29	Column of files from threes... 59
Salutes in march.............. 29	Column of threes from files 59
Support swords................ 29	Column of twos from line.. 60

205

INDEX.

Line from column of twos ... 60
Column of files from line, etc.. 60
Single and double rank.. ... 60
Double rank distance......... 60
Column of Divisions 62
Same and move forward 64
To halt or march column divisions 64
" oblique column divisions... 65
" change direction col. div's. 65
Same and put in march........ 65
" faced and marched to rear.. 66
To form line from column of divisions to or on right, etc.... 67
To form line and continue march 67
" break into divisions........ 68
" re-form Legion 69
" march column divisions by flank and re-form column. 70
To advance by right or left of divisions, and form line again 71, 72
To form threes from col. di'vs. 72
" form Col. Div's. from col 3's 73
LEGION DISPLAY DRILL...... 74
Position and numbers 74
To form column 3's by flank movement from column of files 75
" form line faced to rear from column of threes 75
To form line by two movements from column of threes... 76
To form line faced to the rear by same................... 76
To change front............ ... 77
" form line on standard...... 78
" wheel about standard...... 78
" wheel in line from col. of threes..... 79
To form column sections...... 79
" wheel into sections from line and advance 80
To form column sections from threes.................. 80
To form same right or left from threes 81
To break into col. 3's from col. sections................... 81
To form column threes to right or left from col. sections. 82
To march in line before completion of above... 82
To form col. 3's from col. sec. and march to rear and re-form section..........83, 84
To close sections to ½ distance, etc... 84
To take wheeling distance.... 85
" form col. sec. forward from line 85
To form line to front from sections.................... 86
To form line by 2 movements from col. sections at ½ distance 86
To form line by 3 movements. 87
" form column of 2's from col. of sections 88
To wheel in circles 89
" wheel ½ sections........... 89
" advance even sections, etc 90
" deploy col. sections......91-94
" form double sections from column sections......... . 94
" break into sections......... 95
" wheel subdivisions consecutively.................. 96
" change direction column by flank.. 97
" advance by right or left of double sec................ 98
To break by right of subdivisions rear into columns.98-101
" deploy col. double sec..101-104
" deploy col. 3's open order..104
" deploy col., sections, etc...105
" close the column... 106
" deploy to front by files.....107
" deploy line, open order... 107
" extend and close intervals.108
" counter-march, open order.108
ORDER IN ECHELON..........109
To march echelon to rear.....110
" march echelon by flank....110
" re-form line from echelon..111
" form sections in echelon from threes in echelon....111
" form echelon from col. files.111
" open and close ranks in echelon..... 112
" form line obliquely from files in echelon, etc..113-115
GENERAL REMARKS APROPOS.115
To form column from oblique line 115
" form line from files in echelon... 115
CROSSES—
To form cross from column 3's.116
" reduce cross to column 3's..117

INDEX.

To form and reduce Greek
    cross................117, 118
" form Greek and Passion
    Cross from column threes.119
To display Greek Cross...120, 121
" form Greek Cross from line.122
" form Patriarchal Cross.123–125
" form Cross of Salem.......125
" form St. Andrew's Cross...
   125–127
TRIANGLES—
From column of files.........127
From column threes.......129–132
From column sections 132, 133
To form square 133
" reduce Greek Cross to
    left 135–137
" form Initial letters from col.
    sections................187
" form diamond.......138, 139
SCHOOL OF BATTALION.......140
Remarks—who commands....140
When commands are repeated.141
Rank, Position of Legions....141
Equalizing Legions...........142
Standards 142
Post of Officers...............143
Markers......................144
To form Battalion.............144
" open and close ranks ..146, 147
" dismiss Battalion 148
" march in line.............148
" face to rear; to march to
    rear....................149
" oblique and resume for-
    ward 150
To halt Battalion.............150
" rectify alignments 150
" give general alignment....150
" change direction in line....151
" march by flank............152
" break into col. threes from
    right, etc., to march to
    left, etc..................152
To form line to right, etc......153
Successive formations........153
To form line *on* right, etc.....154
" form line to front.........155
" form line to front, faced to
    rear....................155
" form column sections from
    line... 156
" form line from col. sections.157
" form line to right. etc., from
    column sections..........157
To form col. Legions from line.157

To form column and move for-
    ward 158
To form Legions to rear into
    column from line..........159
To break from right, etc., to
    march to left, etc., from
    line 159
To march column forward, etc.160
" change direction of column.160
" form line on right, etc.....161
" correct alignment........ 161
" form line and move for-
    ward 162
To form line to front from halt 163
" form line to front faced to
    rear....................164
To form line by two move-
    ments...................164
To advance by flank of subdivi-
    sions from line 164
To form line from subdivisions
    when marching by flank
    of subdivisions...........165
To form column of subdivisions
    when marching by flank
    of subdivisions and re-
    verse 165
To form col. threes from col.
    Legions or squadrons... 165
To close column to ½ distance.166
" deploy column 166
" form line to right, etc., from
    column squadrons at ½
    distance 166
To form col. Legions from
    column squadrons....... 167
To change front of Battalion.168
HONORS TO BE PAID BY SELECT
    KNIGHTS 169
Visitations and courtesies.....170
ESCORTS OF HONOR...........171
Reception and escort of a
    Grand Officer............172
DRESS PARADE................173
REVIEW 177
GENERAL PARADE 180
SWORD SIGNALS..............184
BUGLE SIGNALS...............186
AWARD OF PRIZE.............195
CAMPS AND CAMPING........199
The Quartermaster...........201
CORRESPONDENCE AND OR-
    DERS 202
Forms of orders..............203
Forms of endorsement........204

Appendix.

BURIAL SERVICE.

[Prepared by Committee on Burial Rites appointed by the Supreme Legion.]

It is supposed that in every town where there is a Legion of Select Knights, there is also a Lodge of the A. O. U. W., and that this Lodge will claim a prior right to the body of the deceased Comrade and Brother; this Lodge should be allowed to furnish the pall bearers; should the Lodge furnish the pall bearers, the Select Knight pall bearers shall act as a Guard of Honor, taking their position on each side of the pall bearers or the hearse; the Guard of Honor shall be equal in number to that of pall bearers; the Select Commander is requested to consult with the M. W. and P. M. W. of the Lodge in regard to the various duties to be performed by each, so there will be no confusion at the grave.

A Select Knight must perform escort duty at the burial of a Select Knight by his Legion. Upon notice of the death of a Select Knight, it shall be the duty of the Select Commander to notify every Knight of the Legion that he shall appear in full uniform, at a stated hour, at the Hall or usual meeting place, for the purpose of performing escort duty at the funeral of the deceased Comrade.

The Select Commander will preside during the ceremonies, assisted by the Vice and Lieut.-Commanders and Chaplain. The Select Commander having convened the Select Knights of the Legion, they being in full uniform, sword-hilts dressed in mourning, the Legion will be formed in two ranks; pall bearers will be selected and placed on the left of the Legion; the Standard Bearer, with colors draped in mourning, on left of the pall bearers; the Officers of the Legion on left of colors, according to rank; the Senior Workman with sword and belt and the Junior Workman with chapeau of deceased, on the extreme left. The Legion being formed and ready to move, the Select Commander will command:

Legion, ATTENTION,

Marshal, the Legion is now in your hands—lead on.
The Marshal will now command:

Right (or *left*) FACE. *Forward*, MARCH.

The Legion will march to the residence of the deceased. On arriving at the door of the residence, the Marshal will command:

Legion, HALT; *Right and left side step*,' MARCH; *Inward*, FACE.

The Select Commander and Chaplain, followed by the Vice and Lieut.-Commanders, pall bearers, Senior and Junior Workmen, will march between ranks into the house.

The Select Commander, having formally received the remains, the Senior and Junior Workmen will place sword and chapeau on coffin, and the pall bearers range themselves on each side of the coffin; Select Commander will give command: *Form arch*.* (Guard of Honor or pall bearers will now, with their swords, form Arch of Steel over coffin). As soon as emblems are placed on coffin, pall bearers return swords, carry and place coffin in hearse; then take position on each side of hearse, at a *carry swords*.

When the Select Commander has entered the house, the Marshal will command:

Parade, REST.

---

*Same as "*Cross Swords.*"

On the approach of pall bearers, with coffin, he will command:

Legion, ATTENTION. *Carry*, SWORDS. *Present*, SWORDS. *Legion*, UN-COVER.

Remaining thus until coffin is placed in hearse. The Marshal will now command:

Legion, RE-COVER. *Carry*, SWORDS.

As soon as the hearse moves forward the Marshal will command:

By Twos, Inward, Counter-march.

As soon as the Legion is again formed in column of twos or fours (as the strength of the Legion will permit) the Marshal will command:

Reverse, SWORDS. *Forward*, MARCH.

The Select Commander, Vice-Commander, Lieut.-Commander, Standard Bearer, Chaplain and Senior and Junior Workmen in rear of hearse; the Legion will move in same order as at first.

On arriving at the cemetery, the hearse will be halted at Legion distance from the grave. The Marshal will command:

Legion right and left open order. Forward, MARCH.

Head of Legion having reached the grave, he will command:

Legion, HALT. *Inward*, FACE. *Legion*, UN-COVER. *Present*, SWORDS.

Select Commander will direct pall bearers to remove the coffin.

The Select Commander and Chaplain will march at the head of pall bearers; Vice and Lieut.-Commanders, Standard Bearer, Senior and Junior Workmen after pall bearers. The Select Commander and Chaplain will take post at head of grave; pall bearers on each side of grave; Vice and

Lieut.-Commanders, Standard Bearer, Senior and Junior Workmen at foot of grave. As soon as thus formed, the Marshal will command:

Legion, RE-COVER. *Carry,* SWORDS. *Right,* FACE. *Forward,* MARCH.

Legion will now form around the grave. The Marshal will conduct the relatives to the head of the grave, when the Master Workman of the Lodge will open the ceremonies by saying:

"Rest here, fellow-Workmen, for the days of our Brother on earth are ended. We will now consign his remains to the silent tomb, which is the final destination of all alike. We, too, like our Brother, whose remains now lie before us, shall soon be shrouded in the habilaments of death, and our bodies consigned to the narrow house of the dead."

Should the Legion conduct the whole ceremonies, the Marshal will open them by reading or repeating the above paragraph in the A. O. U. W. funeral ceremonies, by saying: "Rest here, Comrades and fellow-Workmen," and etc. When he has finished, the Select Commander will give command:

Guard of Honor, Form, ARCH.

The Guard of Honor, or pall bearers will now form arch over the coffin which is resting over the grave.

S. C.—Comrades, to-day we are called upon to administer the last sad rites to our loved Comrade and Brother, who, having fulfilled his mission among men on earth has left behind him all that is mortal of man, while his spirit has taken its flight to that celestial sphere where our arch of steel can no longer cheer, protect and encourage him, as it has in the past, in his manifold struggles, incident to a pilgrimage in this World of Woe. Our Comrade and Brother aided and assisted us in the elevation of mankind, and in carrying out the Royal Law—as ye would that men should do to you, do ye even so unto them.

By Education he endeavored to gain that intelligent Wisdom for himself and others, which would enable him to stand worthily among the highest and best, having an exalted Reputation founded on a character unstained.

By his industry he strove to do his duty as a Man amongst men in providing for himself and those dependent upon him.

By his union with us he followed the noble dictates of his heart and conscience to labor for the advancement of, and to defend the good of, Society.

In this solemn hour we should remember that while the form of our Comrade and Brother, that now lies so still and cold before us, but a few short hours ago lived as we live; that in his course through life he experienced all of the various feelings of joy and pleasure, and of sorrow and sadness that we experience; that he has only passed on as one of the advance guard for the multitude that shall follow in his wake; and that it is but, a few short moments in the vast space of eternity, until we, too, shall receive the dread summons, to join the innumerable caravan that moves to the pale realms of shade, where each shall take his place in the silent halls of death.

Though the silver thread of life has been broken, the arch of steel under which he is now resting shall watch over, guide and protect all that was near and dear to him in life, in the future as it has in the past.

The Select Commander commands:

Carry, SWORDS. *Parade*, REST.

The body shall now be lowered into the grave, and after religious services of friends, the Past Master of the A. O. U. W. shall resume, and in the absence of P. M. the S. K. Chaplain may take his place.

P. M. W.—A melancholy occasion like this, which calls us now to surround a Brother Workman's grave, and to deposit his remains in the lonely tomb, is, to us, full of profitable instruction, if we would but heed the lesson given us in such a solem manner to-day. Here we are reminded that we, too, are mortal, and like our brother shall soon be wrapped in the winding-sheet of death, and our bodies deposited in the narrow house of the dead.

There is none so rich he cannot die, and none so poor that he cannot find a resting place. Pride and humility, wealth and poverty, all become victims to the iron tooth of time, and under this green sod find a common level. Our Brother is not now of this earth. The oil in his lamp of earthly life became exhausted, its light waned and flickered, and finally became extinguished; but we sincerely hope that his liberated soul may ever drink pure draughts from those never-failing streams of eternal life, which have their fountain-head close to the throne of God.

And now, while we mourn the departure from our midst of a beloved Brother, and drop the tear of sympathy with those whose loss has been greater than ours, let us cherish his memory, and profit by this proof of the Divine will and almighty power.

Let us pray.

Almighty God, Our Heavenly Father—in whom we live, move and have our being; the giver of every good and perfect gift; our only refuge in time of need—we come to thee, in this, our hour of distress. As thou hast seen fit to remove from our midst our beloved Brother, we humbly commit his soul into Thy keeping. We pray Thee, our God, to look with pity upon the sorrowing family and friends of our departed brother. Let them be drawn towards Thee by the tender chords of Thy holy love, and let this severe blow be softened to them by the hope that this separation is not forever; that he has only gone before, and that in a few days, at most they to him will be re-united, where parting shall be no more. We would ask Thee, our Heavenly Father, to bless the institution of which our beloved Brother was a worthy member. May the efforts being put forth by us to inculcate Friendship, Brotherly Love, Truth and Virtue, and to fraternize the world, receive thy approval, and lead us to bow with reverence to Thy holy will, and Thy name shall be praised, now and evermore. Amen.

The A. O. U. W. Burial Ode may now be sung; then the S. K. Chaplain resumes.

BURIAL ODE.

As, bowed by sudden storms, the rose
   Sinks on the garden's breast,
Down to the grave our *Brother* goes,
   In silence there to rest.

No more with us his welcome voice
   The *Mystic* Ode shall swell;
No more his cheerful heart rejoice
   When peals the Sabbath bell.

But far away, in cloudless sphere
   Amid a spotless throng,
He's joining, with celestial voice,
   The everlasting song.

No more we'll mourn our absent friend,
   But lift our earnest prayer—
That when our work in life shall end,
   We all may join him there.

S. K. Chap.—Comrades, Brothers, and Friends, in this dark and trying hour of sorrow and calamity, when we are in the presence of death, should we not pause for a moment and consider what our duties are to our Creator, to ourselves and to those dependent upon us? Should we not search the innermost recess of our hearts and conscience, to discover and expunge those evil thoughts and selfish actions which so pervade our human nature that they retard the high aspirations of the soul? Should we not leave this solemn place with the firm resolve, that from henceforth we shall try to so live, that when the dread summon comes, we may go forth with an unfaltering Trust, and approach our graves like one who wraps the drapery of his couch about him and lies down to pleasant dreams?

We can not come here without subdued hearts and softened affections. When the dark shadow of death approaches our home, every voice is hushed and the conscience instinctively holds communion with the hereafter, and on the mutability of earthly affairs. The sad and solemn scene before you now stirs up these feelings with a force and vivid power heretofore unfelt. He, who now slumbers that last long unbroken and undisturbed sleep of death, was our Comrade and Brother, with whom we have walked the pilgrimage and have shared the pleasures of life, as well as its sorrows. He was born as we were born, he has lived as we live, and he has died as we must die. He is now summoned beyond the effects of praise or censure. That we loved him, our presence here bears testimony; that he had faults is to repeat what his mortality demonstrates, that he was but human, and not Divine. The memory of his virtues lingers in our remembrance, and reflects its shining radiance beyond the portals of the tomb.

The earthen vase which has contained precious odors will lose none of its fragrance, though the clay be broken and shattered; so be it with the memory of our Comrade and Brother.

Let us pray.

Oh, everlasting God, supreme commander and earnest friend of every true and righteous heart. We beseech thee to look with compassionate tenderness on us in this our sad bereavement. Let thy consolation, solace and support, sustain the family of our deceased comrade, and help them and us to so live in thy light, that we may meet with him again in that realm where sorrow and death never enter, and thine shall be the honor and praise forevermore. Amen.

M. W.—Brethern, we stand in the silent city of the dead. Our hearts are sad as we realize that we have gathered here for the purpose of depositing in the cold grave the remains of our beloved brother and comrade. We shall never again, in this life, be privileged to commune and fraternize with him, and look upon his face, or hear his voice, as of old, speaking words of sympathy and encouragement. Oh! what a solemn lesson! Look around you and the evidence of that great truth, that we must all *pass away* and that "the places which now know us shall know us no more again forever." Let us therefore, seriously and solemnly reflect that duty calls us to be ready for the change. Let us not mistake the import of the lesson we are here taught, but interpret it correctly and bind it upon our hearts. God, the all-wise Father, has taken our brother and comrade to himself and he is no longer one of us. We now commit his body to the tomb.

Taking some earth in his hand and sprinkling it upon the coffin, the M. W. will continue:

M. W. — "Earth to earth, dust to dust, ashes to ashes." Rest in peace, and may the spirit soar aloft to join the Supreme Lodge on high, where there is no more sorrow, nor parting, nor death, but everlasting life, full of peace and joy unspeakable, and full of glory. Farewell, my brother, farewell.

All in the procession will repeat—

Farewell.

The procession will now re-form and march back to their hall.

Respectfully submitted in
      E. I. AND U.,
           FRANCIS SENNIGER,
           H. L. DEAM,
           Committee on Funeral Rites.

www.ingramcontent.com/pod-product-compliance
Lightning Source LLC
Chambersburg PA
CBHW020815230426
43666CB00007B/1024